National Parks System Plan

Cover photographs by the author.

© Minister of Supply and Services Canada 1990

Cat. No.   R62-254/1990 E

ISBN No.   0-662-18206-5

Available free of charge through:

Enquiries Centre

Environment Canada

Ottawa, Ontario

K1A 0H3

Printed on recycled paper.

April, 1991

Aussi disponible en français.

PREFACE

Canada's natural environment is a rich mosaic of landscapes and ecosystems, each of which exhibits a characteristic blend of geology, physiography, vegetation and wildlife. This richness is our legacy, our natural heritage. It has molded our history and continues to shape the future of our country.

The goal of Canada's national parks system is to represent and protect the diversity of Canada's natural heritage. The publication of the **"National Parks System Plan"** is a major step towards this goal. It clearly presents the status of the national park system in each of Canada's 39 National Park Natural Regions. But it is more than a status report. It also portrays Canada's natural regions with poetry, photographs and descriptions that weave a vivid tapestry of Canada's landscapes and wildlife.

As a planning tool, status report and portrait of Canada's natural history, this document will be of interest to a wide audience, including students, environmentalists, national park staff, and the general public. It is a statement to all Canadians of the Canadian Park Service's commitment to protect and preserve our national heritage – now and forever.

A/Assistant Deputy Minister
Canadian Parks Service

ACKNOWLEDGEMENTS

A task as complex as that of producing the "National Parks System Plan" clearly demanded a great deal of time, patience and dedication from a number of people. I would like to thank at this time all my collegues in the National Parks Systems Branch who took the time to comment on the various drafts of this document and provided helpful information and suggestions. Several other people deserve special mention. Werner Wicke, Senior Designer, National Historic Parks and Sites, came up with the initial design and edited the visual elements of the document. Lynda Wegner, of Fresh Image, did the page layouts and endured the continual stream of last-minute changes without complaint. Brenda Missen, freelance editor and writer, polished the words and combed out the clichés. Ian Joyce produced all the maps by hand. Andre Guindon provided invaluable assistance in selecting the photographs from the Canadian Park Service's slide collection.

I hope that this book promotes greater understanding and appreciation of our national parks system and that it, in some small way, contributes to the goal of completing a national parks system that truly represents the image of our land and its life.

Max Finkelstein
Project Manager
Writer

TABLE OF CONTENTS

Maps

INTRODUCTION

To protect for all time representative natural areas of Canadian significance in a system of national parks, and to encourage public understanding, appreciation and enjoyment of this natural heritage so as to leave it unimpaired for future generations.

Canadian Parks Service Objective for National Parks

Fundy National Park

CANADA'S NATIONAL HERITAGE

As Canadians, we are increasingly concerned about the environment that will be inherited by our children. In a world of rapid change, our parks and historic sites are seen as models of environmental stewardship and as an important legacy to be preserved for future generations. They represent one of the most tangible and enduring demonstrations of the federal government's commitment to the environment.

The federal government has made a commitment to implement the concept of sustainable development as described in "Our Common Future", the final report of the World Commission on Environment and Development (The Brundtland Report). This concept holds that human economic development must be compatible with the long-term maintenance of natural ecosystems and life support processes. A strategy to implement sustainable development requires not only the careful management of those lands and resources that are exploited to support our economy, but also the protection and presentation of our most important natural and cultural areas. Our system of national parks and national historic sites is one of the nation's – indeed the world's – greatest treasures. It also represents a key resource for the tourism industry in Canada, attracting both domestic and foreign visitors. The

Grasslands National Park

federal government is committed to passing on this priceless legacy not only intact, but expanded and improved.

OUR NATIONAL PARKS

National parks protect major natural environments representative of Canada's natural heritage. These special places are gateways to nature, to adventure, to discovery, to solitude. They celebrate the beauty and infinite variety of our land. Protected and preserved for all Canadians and for the world, each is a sanctuary in which nature is allowed to evolve in its own way, as it has done since the dawn of time. Each provides a haven, not only for plants and animals, but also for the human spirit. A place to wander … to wonder … to discover yourself.

Canada's first national park was created over 100 years ago at Banff. The goal, as expressed in the 1979 policy, is to establish a system of national

parks that represents each of Canada's distinct natural regions. But as national parks enter their second century, this system is just over halfway toward completion.

The purpose of this report is to familiarize the reader with the 39 terrestrial natural regions of Canada (Map 1), to identify the regions already represented by national parks and to introduce those regions still needing national parks. The status of completion of the national parks system is shown on Map 2. More detail is provided in the descriptions of the natural regions. This information is summarized in Appendix 1.

Pacific Rim National Park

IT STARTED AT BANFF …

National parks are part of a grand vision to preserve examples of the diversity of our land and of the life that is an integral part of it. Commercial resource extraction and sport hunting are not permitted in national parks. But these are not merely nature sanctuaries preserved and

Banff, 1887

By 1911, five national parks in the Rocky and Selkirk mountains had been created. Meanwhile, in the east, other parks were being established, again on federal lands. St. Lawrence Islands National Park was created in 1904 with the reservation of nine islands. Point Pelee was established in 1918 and Georgian Bay Islands in 1929. From 1930 to 1970, attention turned to Atlantic Canada, where five national parks were established by agreement with the provinces for the transfer of the lands to the federal government.

By 1970, 19 national parks had been established, but not according to any real system. They represented, rather, a collection of special places – created in some cases by heroic efforts, accidents of geography or political opportunism – that had been set aside for a variety of purposes that included protecting scenic areas for national and international tourist resorts, providing regional recreation areas, preserving habitat for wildlife, stimulating flagging economies in areas of chronic underemployment … There was no vision or long-term goal for a system of national parks.

locked away; they are places where people of all ages are invited to experience the outdoors and to learn about the natural environment.

The vision began, albeit a much different vision then, in 1885 when the federal government reserved "from sale or settlement or squatting" 26 square kilometres around the hot mineral springs near what is now the town of Banff, Alberta. Two workers constructing the transcontinental railway in this area had discovered the hot springs flowing from a mountainside near the railway station. Various conflicting claims were brought to the attention of the Government of Canada. Rather than grant the privilege of developing the hot springs to private individuals, the government of Sir John A. Macdonald decided instead to retain the hot springs and surrounding lands as a national possession. The Order-in Council, signed two weeks after the driving of the famous last spike that marked the completion of the Canadian Pacific trans-continental railway, signalled the birth of Banff National Park and the system of national parks across Canada.

Two years later, in 1887, the Rocky Mountains Park Act officially set aside the Banff Hot Springs Reserve, enlarged to 405 square kilometres, as a "public park and pleasure ground for the benefit, advantage and enjoyment of the people of Canada."

A SYSTEM PLAN FOR NATIONAL PARKS

This vision of a system of parks was provided by a national parks plan devised in the early 1970s. Its fundamental principle was to protect an outstanding representative sample of each of Canada's landscapes and natural phenomena. In order to guide the development of a finite system of national parks using this principle of "representativeness", the plan divided Canada into 39 distinct "National Park Natural Regions" based on physiography and vegetation. The goal is to represent each natural region in the national parks system. This approach has provided a policy framework as well as a goal which has guided the expansion of the national parks system since that time.

St. Croix Canadian Heritage River

When the system is complete, future generations will be able to experience in our national parks the biophysical diversity of Canada – examples of the Pacific coast, the Rockies, the prairie grasslands, the boreal plains, the tundra hills, the Precambrian shield, the Arctic Islands, the Atlantic coast and each of the other distinctive natural landscapes that comprise our natural heritage and which have shaped our history.

To date, 21 natural regions are represented by the 34 national parks and national park reserves in the system. (Several natural regions, including the Rocky Mountains, contain more than one national park.) The main gaps in the system are in the Northwest Territories, Quebec, Labrador, Manitoba and British Columbia. National parks currently occupy 1.9 percent of Canada; and when the system is complete they will likely cover about 2.8 percent.

National parks are not the only protected natural areas in Canada. They are part of a broader family of Canadian heritage lands that includes provincial and territorial parks, wildlife areas, heritage rivers, regional parks, ecological reserves and lands under private stewardship (see Table I, Appendix 1). The international significance of some of these has been recognized through their designation as World Heritage Sites or Biosphere Reserves. But national parks occupy a special place among our heritage lands as the system protected for the benefit, education and enjoyment of all Canadians under legislation of the Parliament of Canada.

HOW DO NEW NATIONAL PARKS COME INTO BEING?

National parks are a special type of public lands administered by the federal government under the provisions of the National Parks Act. Identifying, selecting and establishing new national parks can be a long and complex process.

No fixed or standard process exists by which new national parks are created. Each situation is different, and the final result reflects the individual circumstances and the involvement of all those parties that are directly affected. The following paragraphs give an overview and outline of the normal sequence of events.

Map 1: National Park Natural Regions

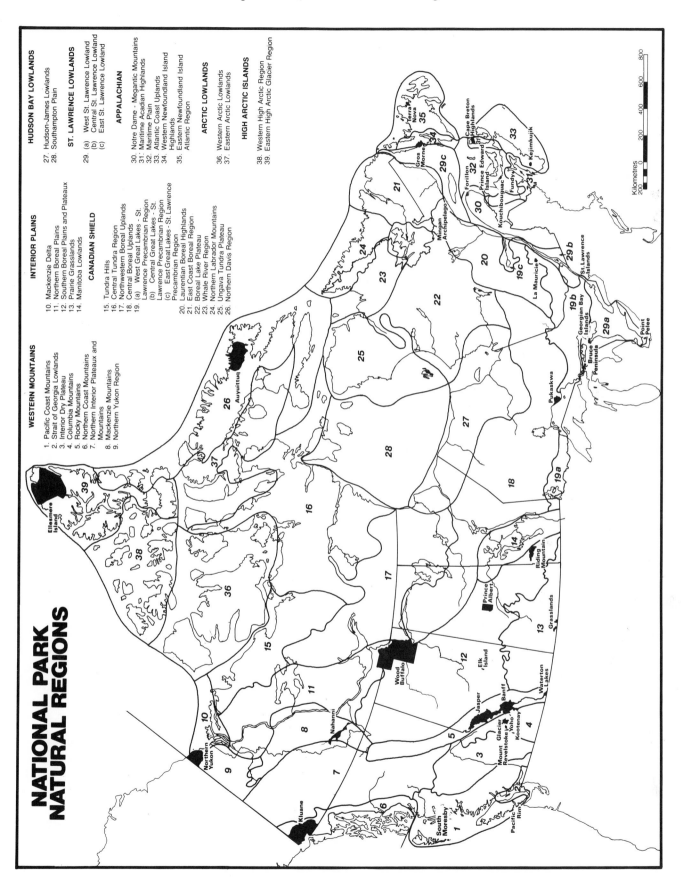

NATIONAL PARK NATURAL REGIONS

WESTERN MOUNTAINS
1. Pacific Coast Mountains
2. Strait of Georgia Lowlands
3. Interior Dry Plateau
4. Columbia Mountains
5. Rocky Mountains
6. Northern Coast Mountains
7. Northern Interior Plateaux and Mountains
8. Mackenzie Mountains
9. Northern Yukon Region

INTERIOR PLAINS
10. Mackenzie Delta
11. Northern Boreal Plains
12. Southern Boreal Plains and Plateaux
13. Prairie Grasslands
14. Manitoba Lowlands

CANADIAN SHIELD
15. Tundra Hills
16. Central Tundra Region
17. Northwestern Boreal Uplands
18. Central Boreal Uplands
19. (a) West Great Lakes - St. Lawrence Precambrian Region
    (b) Central Great Lakes - St. Lawrence Precambrian Region
    (c) East Great Lakes - St. Lawrence Precambrian Region
20. Laurentian Boreal Highlands
21. East Coast Boreal Region
22. Boreal Lake Plateau
23. Whale River Region
24. Northern Labrador Mountains
25. Ungava Tundra Plateau
26. Northern Davis Region

HUDSON BAY LOWLANDS
27. Hudson-James Lowlands
28. Southampton Plain

ST. LAWRENCE LOWLANDS
29. (a) West St. Lawrence Lowland
    (b) Central St. Lawrence Lowland
    (c) East St. Lawrence Lowland

APPALACHIAN
30. Notre Dame - Megantic Mountains
31. Maritime Acadian Highlands
32. Maritime Plain
33. Atlantic Coast Uplands
34. Western Newfoundland Island Highlands
35. Eastern Newfoundland Island Atlantic Region

ARCTIC LOWLANDS
36. Western Arctic Lowlands
37. Eastern Arctic Lowlands

HIGH ARCTIC ISLANDS
38. Western High Arctic Region
39. Eastern High Arctic Glacier Region

Kilometres
200 400 600 800

Map 2: Status of National Park Natural Regions

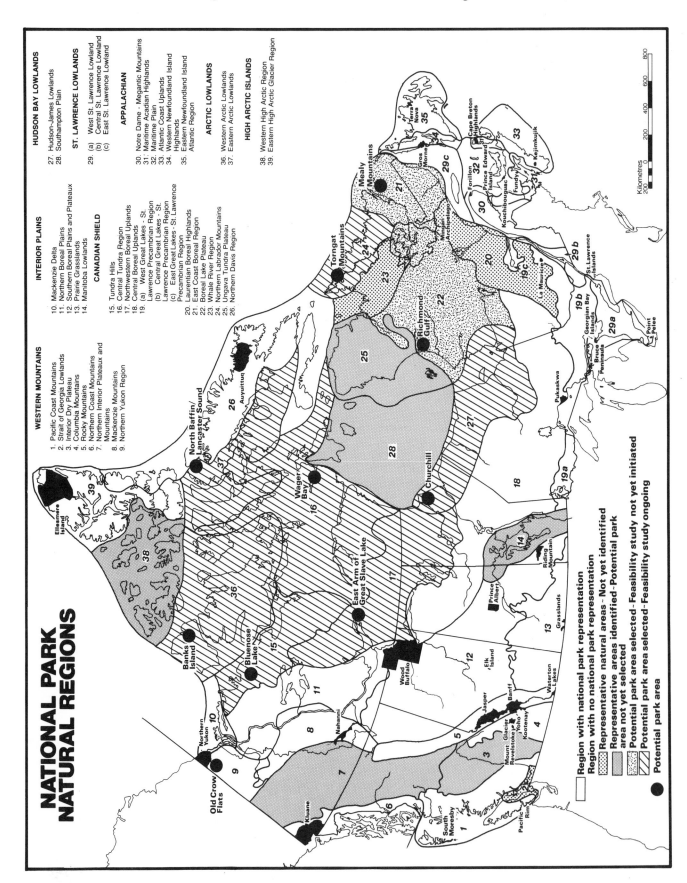

NATIONAL PARK NATURAL REGIONS

WESTERN MOUNTAINS
1. Pacific Coast Mountains
2. Strait of Georgia Lowlands
3. Interior Dry Plateau
4. Columbia Mountains
5. Rocky Mountains
6. Northern Coast Mountains
7. Northern Interior Plateaux and Mountains
8. Mackenzie Mountains
9. Northern Yukon Region

INTERIOR PLAINS
10. Mackenzie Delta
11. Northern Boreal Plains
12. Southern Boreal Plains and Plateaux
13. Prairie Grasslands
14. Manitoba Lowlands

CANADIAN SHIELD
15. Tundra Hills
16. Central Tundra Region
17. Northwestern Boreal Uplands
18. Central Boreal Uplands
19. (a) West Great Lakes - St. Lawrence Precambrian Region
    (b) Central Great Lakes - St. Lawrence Precambrian Region
    (c) East Great Lakes - St. Lawrence Precambrian Region
20. Laurentian Boreal Highlands
21. East Coast Boreal Region
22. Boreal Lake Plateau
23. Whale River Region
24. Northern Labrador Mountains
25. Ungava Tundra Plateau
26. Northern Davis Region

HUDSON BAY LOWLANDS
27. Hudson-James Lowlands
28. Southampton Plain

ST. LAWRENCE LOWLANDS
29. (a) West St. Lawrence Lowland
    (b) Central St. Lawrence Lowland
    (c) East St. Lawrence Lowland

APPALACHIAN
30. Notre Dame - Megantic Mountains
31. Maritime Acadian Highlands
32. Maritime Plain
33. Atlantic Coast Uplands
34. Western Newfoundland Island Highlands
35. Eastern Newfoundland Island Atlantic Region

ARCTIC LOWLANDS
36. Western Arctic Lowlands
37. Eastern Arctic Lowlands

HIGH ARCTIC ISLANDS
38. Western High Arctic Region
39. Eastern High Arctic Glacier Region

Region with national park representation

Region with no national park representation

Representative natural areas - Not yet identified

Representative areas identified - Potential park area not yet selected

Potential park area selected - Feasibility study not yet initiated

Potential park area selected - Feasibility study ongoing

● Potential park area

Kilometres
200 0 200 400 600 800

Identifying Representative Natural Areas:

Because the goal is to represent each of Canada's 39 terrestrial natural regions in the national parks system, efforts to create new parks are concentrated on those natural regions that do not have a national park. In these regions, studies are carried out to identify areas worth consideration. To qualify, such areas must first contain a good representation of the natural features and processes characterizing the region, including its wildlife, vegetation, geology and landforms. The second criterion is that human impact should be minimal; that is, the area should be in a natural state, or be capable of being restored to this condition.

Churchill, proposed national park

- accessibility
- educational value
- competing incompatible land uses
- actual and potential threats to the environment
- presence of other protected areas (e.g., provincial parks)
- land ownership
- the implications of aboriginal claims and treaties
- potential for sustainable tourism development
- national and local public support

East Arm of Great Slave Lake, proposed national park

Selecting Potential Park Areas:

Once representative natural areas have been identified in a natural region, further studies and consultations are undertaken to select one of these areas as a potential national park. In comparing possible areas at this stage, a wide range of factors is considered, including:
- quality of natural region representation
- exceptional natural features
- cultural heritage features
- provincial/territorial government priorities
- opportunities for outdoor recreation

Assessing Park Feasibility:

When a potential park area has been selected for the natural region, a new park proposal is prepared as the basis for a detailed feasibility assessment including public consultations. The factors listed above are now studied in greater detail, usually with the direct involvement of the provincial or territorial government and in consultation with representatives of local communities. Alternative land uses are sometimes explicitly considered and compared and, on lands under federal administration, a Mineral and Energy Resources Assessment is undertaken. Possible boundaries of the potential national park are drawn to include critical wildlife habitats and to incorporate ecological units whose long-term protection is feasible. If this assessment shows that a national park is feasible and that there is public support for this land use option, the governments may decide to proceed with negotiation of a park agreement.

Northern Baffin Island, proposed national park

- final park boundaries
- cost-sharing for land acquisition
- timing of land transfer
- continuation of traditional renewable resource harvesting
- co-operation in park planning and management
- regional integration
- economic benefits

Establishing a New National Park in Legislation:

Once the responsible parties have agreed to create a new park with the lands to be administered by the federal government, the proposed new national park must be formally established by legislation of the Parliament of Canada so that the National Parks Act and Regulations apply. In areas affected by a Comprehensive Native Land Claim, a national park reserve is established. The Act and Regulations apply, but traditional native hunting, trapping and fishing may continue. Final boundaries will only be established on resolution of the claims.

NEW NATIONAL PARKS AND ABORIGINAL PEOPLE

Many of the natural regions not yet represented in the national park system are in the Yukon, Northwest Territories or in the northern parts of the provinces. These are often areas in which aboriginal people continue to rely on renewable resources and in which native cultures reflect a close relationship to the land.

For many years, aboriginal communities expressed strong concerns about the implications of establishing new national parks in areas of traditional native use:
- are national park reserves created without prejudicing native land claims?
- would traditional native uses continue?

If a national park is not a feasible option, other representative natural areas are considered elsewhere in the natural region.

Negotiating a New Park Agreement:

For the federal legislation to apply, it is a constitutional requirement that national park lands must be federal government property. Within the provinces, where the provincial governments administer most lands, a federal-provincial agreement is usually negotiated whereby the province transfers administration and control of the land to the federal government for a new national park. Within the northern territories, it is the practice to seek the concurrence of the territorial government for a new national park through negotiation of a federal-territorial agreement. Where lands are subject to a comprehensive land claim by aboriginal people, a new park can be established as part of a negotiated claim settlement or a national park reserve can be established pending the resolution of the claim.

New park agreements cover many different topics depending on the circumstances. These include:

- would local people be directly involved in management?
- would logging and other commercial resource extraction activities be prohibited?
- would the extent of recreation be controlled through a park management plan?
- would local communities derive economic benefits?

The experience in northern parks and reserves over the past 15 years has shown that the answer to these questions is "yes". New national parks are often a good way to meet the objectives of native communities while protecting and presenting a special place for all Canadians. The Canadian Parks Service will continue to seek co-operative arrangements and to involve aboriginal people in the future of our national parks system.

Pitseolak, Auyuittuq National Park Reserve

opportunity to create new national parks with the direct involvement of native people.

The future of our national parks is being addressed as part of the federal government's environmental action plan ("The Green Plan"). In the spring of 1990, the government proposed to establish at least five new national parks by 1995 and to continue planning to meet its commitment to complete the national parks system.

This report is a key step in charting the course toward that goal, focusing as it does on the status of natural region representation across the country. It should be noted, however, that not all the existing national parks provide the same quality of representation.

Moreover, maintaining the ecological integrity of the parks is becoming increasingly difficult as a result of the pressures of adjacent commercial resource exploitation, transboundary external pollution, global climate change and, in some cases, visitor use. (These factors are the subject of a biennial "State of the Parks" report to Parliament.)

COMPLETING THE SYSTEM

As national parks enter their second century of existence, establishment of new national parks is becoming increasingly complex, expensive and time-consuming. Filling the remaining gaps in the system will not be easy. Little land exists now in Canada that does not have some kind of interest or commitment for uses such as oil and gas development, mining, hydro-electricity, forestry, agriculture and private recreation. Land-use and jurisdictional conflicts will have to be resolved in co-operation with the provinces and territories, and the concerns of local residents will have to be addressed. In many natural regions the resolution of comprehensive land claims presents an

Completion of the national parks system will not be achieved by the federal government acting alone. It will require a new consensus and determination on the part of all Canadians and all levels of government, and a recognition of the important contribution that national parks make toward the quality of our environment and the quality of our lives.

NATURAL REGION DESCRIPTIONS

THE NATURAL REGION MAPS:

Note that the 39 natural region maps that follow are drawn at a scale of 1 cm = 200 km. Existing national parks and reserves are coloured dark green; potential park areas are depicted as light green.

1 Pacific Coast Mountains

Represented by: Pacific Rim National Park Reserve;
South Moresby/Gwaii Hanaas National Park Reserve

WILD AND WET

It is from the land we get our strength, from the sea we get our energy.

Diane Brown (Kwakanat)
Haida Community Health Worker

West Coast Trail, Pacific Rim National Park Reserve

THE LAND:

The biggest trees, the most rainfall, the longest and deepest fiords ... this region is known for Canadian superlatives. A distinctive climate and lofty mountains make this natural region stand alone, like an island, with unique plant and animal communities and living conditions.

In few other natural regions of Canada can one swim or walk through such a diversity of habitats, or experience such a variety of life, in so short a distance – from undersea kelp forests through lush rain forests to alpine tundra and mountain-top glaciers. The Coast Mountains cover most of the region, rising steeply from the fiords and channels. Mount Waddington, the highest

mountain in British Columbia, is over 4000 metres. Glaciers and snowfields cap the tallest ranges. The mountains of Vancouver Island and the Queen Charlottes, although not high, make up in ruggedness what they lack in elevation. The Estevan Coastal Plain, a long narrow strip of rocky coastline, indented, wave-battered and wind-scoured, is a unique landscape found only along the west coast of Vancouver Island.

The most striking feature of this region is the maze of fiords and channels that dissect the coastline from Vancouver to Alaska. These are classic fiords, some of the world's longest and deepest. They slash inland up to 190 kilometres, with sheer sides plunging over 2000 metres. The deepest fiord in the world is Findlayson Channel, with soundings of over 418 fathoms (795 metres).

The region lies within the Pacific Ring of Fire, a portion of the globe known for high volcanic and earthquake activity caused by the movement of crustal plates. Hot springs that beckon backcountry explorers bear testimony to crustal "hot spots" found throughout this region.

Long Beach, Pacific Rim National Park Reserve

VEGETATION:

The combination of heavy rainfall and year-round mild temperatures have resulted in some of the most spectacular temperate rain forests in the world. Here are the most productive forests, the biggest trees and some of the oldest trees in Canada – the Red Creek fir, a massive Douglas fir with a circumference of over 14 metres and a

![South Moresby Island/Gwaii Haanas National Park Reserve]

South Moresby Island/Gwaii Haanas National Park Reserve

height of 80 metres, possibly Canada's biggest tree; the largest western red cedar, 20 metres in circumference, found on Meares Island; Carmanah Creek, site of the world's tallest sitka spruce (95 metres); Cathedral Grove, dominated by Douglas fir as tall in feet as they are old in years - up to 250 feet (85 metres). Yet these are mere babes compared to many western red cedars, which can be over two millennia old.

Three main types of vegetation occur in Natural Region 1. The Coastal Western Hemlock zone occurs up to about 600 metres above sea level. Douglas fir, sitka spruce, western red cedar and western hemlock are the dominant species in this zone. Between 600 metres and 900 metres above sea level is the sub-alpine mountain hemlock zone dominated by mountain hemlock and yellow

cedar. As the elevation increases, the green cloak of evergreen forest begins to break up into krummholz - stunted clumps of trees. Above 900 metres is the third vegetation zone – treeless alpine tundra.

WILDLIFE:

The mainland coast of Natural Region 1 is a stronghold for grizzly bears, which feed heavily on salmon migrating to their spawning streams. Cougar, wolf, blackbear, martin, black-tailed deer (a sub-species of mule deer), wapiti, mountain goat, California bighorn sheep, wolverine and fisher are some of the larger denizens of this region.

Several endemic sub-species and species of wildlife have evolved on the islands of this region: the Vancouver Island marmot, found only in alpine meadows on Vancouver Island; the "blond" or "kermodei" bear, a pale sub-species of black bear found on a few north coastal islands; the Roosevelt elk, among others.

Bald Eagle

Some of these endemics are rare or endangered; some, such as the Dawson caribou, once confined to Graham Island, are now extinct.

The marine environment of this region supports an abundance of life unrivalled in

Canada. Many seabirds, including the mysterious marbled murrelet, nest along the coast of this region. Bald eagles are also commonly seen along the coast. The region's estuaries and fiords provide critical habitat for countless migrating shorebirds and waterfowl, including the trumpeter swan and sandhill crane.

STATUS OF NATIONAL PARKS:

This region is represented by **Pacific Rim National Park Reserve** (500 km²)and **South Moresby/Gwaii Haanas National Park Reserve** (1740 km²).

Pacific Rim National Park Reserve, representing the Estevan Coastal Plain portion of this region, is divided into three distinct units: Long Beach, a strip of uninterrupted surf-pounded beach backed by rain forest and including a marine component extending to the 10-fathom line; the Broken Group Islands, consisting of over 100 islands in a 106-square-kilometre marine component; and a narrow strip along 77 kilometres of coastline that includes the challenging West Coast Trail and an inland wilderness watershed known as the Nitinat Triangle. The first federal-provincial agreement for the establishment of the park was signed in 1970. A final agreement was signed in 1987. Because the area is subject to the comprehensive claim of the Nuu-chah-nulth, it will be proclaimed as a national park reserve under the National Parks Act pending the resolution of this claim.

South Moresby/Gwaii Haanas National Park Reserve, encompassing the rain forests and alpine meadows of the southern Queen Charlotte Islands, harbours 39 species of plants and animals not found anywhere else on the globe. Gwaii Haanas, which means "islands of wonder and beauty", is the Haida name for this wilderness archipelago of 138 islands. Accessible only by boat or aircraft, this diverse area is home to over one-quarter of B.C.'s nesting seabirds, high concentrations of

bald eagles and peregrine falcons, and Canada's largest sea lion rookery. Vegetation varies from endemic plants of the alpine meadows of the rugged San Cristoval Mountains to the towering sitka spruce of coastal rain forests. The interplay of land and marine environments, coupled with the abundance of Haida heritage features, distinguishes this park reserve. The Haida legacy includes the historical village of Ninstints on Anthony Island, a UNESCO cultural World Heritage Site, as well as over 100 inventoried archaeological sites of an estimated total in excess of 450.

A federal-provincial agreement was signed in 1988 committing Canada and British Columbia to create a national park and, by 1992, to set the boundaries for a national marine park. Recognizing that the area falls within the Haida comprehensive claim, negotiations are being undertaken with the Council of the Haida Nation toward an agreement for sharing in the planning,

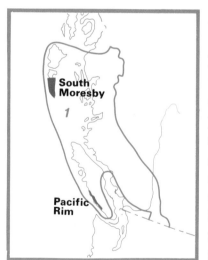

operation and management of the archipelago. The National Parks Act will be amended to establish a national park reserve consistent with the above-mentioned agreements once the initial lands have been transferred from the province.

2 Strait of Georgia Lowlands

Not represented

Gulf Islands

LIFE IN THE RAINSHADOW

Tucked under the rainshadow of the mountains of Vancouver Island and Washington's Olympic Peninsula, this region basks in a balmy Mediterranean climate. Warm dry summers and mild winters that rarely see snow, a frieze of islands and a fertile sea combine to create habitats found nowhere else in Canada.

THE LAND:

From the air, the flat plains of the Fraser Delta and the southern corner of Vancouver Island stand out from the forests, mountains and glaciers that fence them in: a mosaic of rectangular fields, two major cities with spreading suburbs, roads, towns, hydro lines and a spattering of green and brown islands in the blue waters of Georgia Strait. This is one of the most urbanized natural regions in Canada.

Gulf Islands

VEGETATION:

The vegetation of this area is, in a word, unusual. Arbutus, with its constantly shredding smooth red bark, leathery evergreen leaves and twisted, muscular form; Garry oak, gnarled, dark and rough – these species are found nowhere else in Canada. Prickly pear cactus are abundant on some of the Gulf Islands. The dominant vegetation is more familiar – coastal Douglas fir, grandfir, western red cedar, lodgepole pine, Pacific

dogwood (British Columbia's provincial flower), bigleaf maple and red alder.

WILDLIFE:

Many species are found only in this region in Canada and are at the northern most limits of their ranges here – Bendires shrew, California bat, Townsend's chipmunk, Douglas squirrel and western spotted skunk, among many others. Black-tailed deer, a sub-species of mule deer, are the most conspicuous large mammal and are abundant throughout the region.

At the bottom of Active Pass

The mud flats and salt marshes of the Fraser Estuary are critical areas for waterfowl and shorebirds. Millions of migrants flock

– 14 –

here each year, feeding and resting before completing their journeys. Hundreds of thousands spend the winter. Alaksen Migratory Bird Sanctuary, covering 5.2 square kilometres of the Fraser Delta, is of such significance that it has been listed as a Ramsar site– a wetland of international importance. It is one of thirty such sites in Canada.

Pacific Cormorants

STATUS OF NATIONAL PARKS:

No national parks exist yet in this natural region. A regional analysis study to identify representative natural areas will be the first step. However, given the level of development and private ownership, it may be necessary to consider innovative approaches to representing this region in the national parks system.

Establishment of a national park in this natural region will require the concurrence of the Government of British Columbia and local residents.

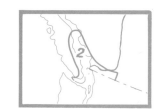

The following table summarizes the status of system planning for each step toward establishing a new national park in this natural region.

At the bottom of Active Pass

Steps in the Park Establishment Process	Status
Representative Natural Areas Identified:	0
Potential Park Area Selected:	0
Park Feasibility Assessed:	0
Park Agreement Signed:	0
Scheduled under the National Parks Act :	0

3 Interior Dry Plateau

Not represented

LAND BETWEEN THE MOUNTAINS

Sandwiched between the Coast Mountains to the west and the Columbia and Rocky Mountains to the east, the Interior Dry Plateau is one of Canada's most diverse natural regions. Choose your clothes carefully for a hike here – within a few miles you can walk from parched "almost-deserts" through moist sub-alpine forests to arctic conditions.

Prickly Pear Cactus

Chilcotin River Valley

THE LAND:

This natural region is characterized by flat or rolling plains, the result of immense lava outpourings 60 million years ago. The plains are dissected by deep narrow valleys, gorges and long, narrow lakes. Hell's Gate, famous with rafters on the Fraser River, is the best known of the river gorges typical of this region.

Lying in the rainshadow of the Coast and Cascade ranges, the region basks under almost guaranteed summer sun. In the parched bottomlands, the temperature can rise to an oven-like 35 degrees Celsius or more.

VEGETATION:

In the deepest valleys where the rainshadow effect is strongest is a mosaic of open ponderosa pine forests, sagebrush and bunchgrass. This is cowboy country, an almost-desert unique in Canada, where cactus, sagebrush, bitterroot, bitterbush and other species thrive. Above the open rangelands, forests of Douglas fir darken the higher plateau country. At still higher elevations, on moister slopes, is a narrow band where Engelmann spruce and alpine fir are the climax species. As a result of past fires, lodgepole pine is now the most common species in this zone. Finally, at the highest elevations, patches of alpine tundra cover the mountain slopes.

WILDLIFE:

The Interior Dry Plateau is home to a host of creatures that slither, scuttle, hop, run, glide and hover in the driest, deepest desert-like valleys: the pygmy horned lizard, western blue-tailed skink, tailed frog, Great Basin Spadefoot Toad, alligator lizard, rubber boa, yellowed-bellied racer, canyon wren, white-throated swift, white-headed woodpecker, black-chinned hummingbird (Canada's smallest bird), and California bighorn sheep. Scorpions and rattlesnakes are also encountered. And, of course, Lake Okanogan is the haunt of Ogopogo, Canada's most famous, but as yet unauthenticated, lake monster. These species, uncommon in Canada outside of Natural Region 3, share the region with more familiar creatures such as grizzly bears, mountain goats, wolverines, mountain caribou, badgers, white-tailed jackrabbits and cougars.

Cougar

The almost-deserts of the driest valley bottoms – and their associated species – are among the rarest and most threatened habitats in Canada. Cattle ranching, sheep grazing and cultivation have already modified much of these arid habitats and reduced the populations of species already limited in number.

STATUS OF NATIONAL PARKS:

No national parks have yet been established in this region. Two representative natural areas have been identified: **Churn Creek** and **Fraser-Chilcotin Junction.** These contiguous areas include roaring wild rivers, large herds of California bighorn sheep, and spectacular canyons and gullies. The next step will be to consider with the provincial government whether one of these areas should be selected for further study as a potential national park.

Factors that could influence new park establishment include several ongoing land uses that are incompatible with national park purposes – logging, ranching, agriculture (fruit-tree orchards, along with other types of farming) and military training. Much of the land is privately owned. The Alkali Lake comprehensive land claim could overlap these representative natural areas. This claim is not currently being negotiated. Establishment of a national park in this natural region will require the support and co-operation of the Government of British Columbia and local residents.

The following table summarizes the status of system planning for each step toward establishing a new national park in this natural region.

Steps in the Park Establishment Process	Status
Representative Natural Areas Identified:	Done
Potential Park Area Selected:	0
Park Feasibility Assessed:	0
Park Agreement Signed:	0
Scheduled Under the National Parks Act :	0

4   Columbia Mountains

Represented by: Mt. Revelstoke National Park; Glacier National Park

Avalanche Paths, Glacier National Park

IN THE LAND OF UP AND DOWN

…station and Hotel are within thirty minutes' walking distance of the Illecillewaet Glacier, from which, at the left, Sir Donald (10,808 ft.) rises a naked and abrupt pyramid …

From an early CPR tourist brochure describing Glacier House amid the "Alps of North America"

Mount Revelstoke National Park

THE LAND:

A vertical world of narrow valleys and canyons squeezed between sheer mountain walls. This region has up to 23 metres of snowfall each year, triggering avalanches and spawning glaciers and icefields. In the north and central areas, the ranges are wild, jagged and spectacularly rugged, contrasting with the rounded tamer summits, forested to the top, that prevail in the south.

Hot springs are a feature of the major valleys.

VEGETATION:

This is interior rain forest country. This region has the greatest diversity of coniferous tree species in Canada, and the productivity of its forests is surpassed only by the coastal rain forests.

At low to middle elevations are luxuriant forests of western red cedar and western hemlock. Alpine larch adds a splash of gold to the uniform green-black of the forest in autumn.

Above the wet forest, dense stands of Engelmann spruce, alpine fir and lodgepole pine predominate up to the alpine tundra. A brilliant palette of colour – Indian paintbrush, lupine, arnica and other species – paint the lush green alpine meadows with burning red, fiery orange, electric blue....

WILDLIFE:

Here is a region where large mammals are still plentiful and where visitors are afforded many fine opportunities for big-game viewing. Most of the mammals of the western mountains are found here. Grizzly and black bear forage on the lush vegetation of avalanche slopes; mountain goats can be seen on sheer cliffs while slightly less daring bighorn sheep graze on steep slopes. Mule deer, white-tailed deer, elk and moose share the forests with wolves and cougar. Pikas, mantled ground squirrels, hoary marmots and lemmings forage in the alpine meadows. The mountain caribou is disappearing from the region as mature forests are clear-cut.

STATUS OF NATIONAL PARKS:

Two national parks represent this region, **Glacier** (1349 km^2) and **Mount Revelstoke** (260 km^2).

These parks preserve a sample of the rugged Columbia Mountains. Their sharp peaks, avalanche-scarred slopes and sheets of perpetual ice and snow make these among the most rugged parks in western Canada. Over half of their area is above the tree line, a stark world of ice and rock. Heavy precipitation falls on these parks, creating a lush forest of western red cedar and western hemlock in the valleys and feeding over 400 glaciers, some of which are visible from the highway. Plentiful snow and steep slopes combine to make these parks active avalanche areas. The many avalanche slopes provide excellent forage for both black and grizzly bears. Nakimu Cave in Glacier National Park, the second biggest cave system in Canada (next in size to Castleguard Cave in Banff National Park), is an underground fantasyland of "moon-milk", black pools and hidden waterfalls.

Mount Revelstoke

Glacier National Park was established around Rogers Pass in 1886, a year after the Canadian Pacific Railway line had crossed the pass. With access provided by the CPR line, the spectacular mountain scenery and fine opportunities for skiing and mountaineering in this area attracted wealthy visitors before the turn of the century. North American mountaineering had its beginnings in Glacier National Park, and Mt. Revelstoke is generally acknowledged as the birthplace of alpine skiing in Canada. Mount Revelstoke National Park was established in 1914 after a group of citizens, impressed with its alpine flowers and mountain scenery, lobbied the federal government to preserve the area.

Mount Revelstoke **Glacier**

4

5   Rocky Mountains

Represented by: Jasper National Park; Banff National Park; Yoho National Park; Kootenay National Park; and Waterton Lakes National Park

ROCKY MOUNTAIN HIGH! ... SEABEDS IN THE SKY

Glistening snow-capped peaks and thundering waterfalls, bugling elk and whistling marmots, lakes of startling turquoise and ice-blue glaciers – this natural region is postcard country. Within this region is some of the most famous and familiar mountain scenery in the world.

Mount Rundle, Banff National Park

THE LAND:

This region encompasses a series of parallel ranges including the Rocky Mountains and the foothills. These are orderly mountains, with wide sweeping valleys separating the ranges and open pine forests cloaking their shoulders. The sedimentary rocks making up the mountains of this region, lifted and folded, sculpted by glaciers and rushing water, have resulted in distinctive, angular peaks. Many peaks exceed 3000 metres with Mt. Robson, at 3954 metres, the highest.

VEGETATION:

Dramatic climate variation caused by elevation, rainshadow effects and latitude create a complex, diverse pattern of vegetation ranging from grasslands and alpine meadows to towering forests of evergreens. But the most dominant vegetation is the sub-alpine forest. This is a high forest, spreading down valleys below alpine meadows like a black tide. It can be an open, sunlit easy-to-walk-through forest typified by lodgepole pine or a dark, dense and damp forest of sharp-pointed Engelmann spruce and alpine fir. Alpine larch provide brilliant yellow patches of colour each autumn. Montane grasslands cover large areas.

WILDLIFE:

This region is famous for its easily observed wildlife. In long-established parks such as Banff and Jasper, the wildlife has learned to tolerate and,

Waterton Lakes National Park

Big Horn Sheep

in some cases to exploit, people, making these parks the premier place in North America for mammal-watching. A drive along the highways traversing the national parks almost guarantees sightings of moose, elk, mule deer, bighorn sheep, mountain goats, black bear or coyote. The region is also known for its game fish. Many species of trout, including non-native species such as brook and brown trout, thrive in the region's cold water rivers and streams alongside native rainbow, cutthroat and Dolly Varden.

STATUS OF NATIONAL PARKS:

Canada's national parks system has its beginnings in this region over 100 years ago with the creation of a 26-square-kilometre national reserve around hot sulphur springs discovered near Banff. Since then, this reserve has grown to an area of 6641 square kilometres and become known as **Banff National Park**. **Yoho** (1313 km²) and **Waterton Lakes** (505km²) were established by the federal government in 1886 and 1895 respectively; **Jasper** (10 878 km²) in 1907; and **Kootenay** (1406 km²)in 1920.

Today, the five national parks protect more than 12 percent of the region's area, providing representation of the geology, vegetation and wildlife of the Rocky Mountains. Waterton Lakes National Park is linked with Montana's Glacier National Park as Waterton-Glacier International Peace Park. This national park forms the core area of the Waterton Biosphere Reserve, one of six biosphere reserves in Canada.

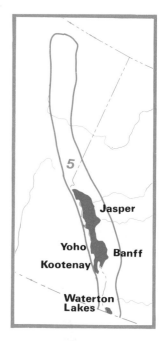

The contiguous block of Banff, Jasper, Kootenay and Yoho national parks, augmented by several provincial parks and wilderness areas on its periphery, is the largest protected area in the mountains of North America. These four parks were declared a World Heritage Site in 1985 because of their exceptional geological features and unspoiled beauty.

The sedimentary strata of the mountains — ancient seabeds compressed into rock and thrust into the sky — bear witness to events from a billion years ago to the age of mammals, the most complete sequence of sedimentary rocks found in Canada. The Burgess Shale Formation in Yoho National Park contains a remarkably preserved record of sea life from over 500 million years ago.

Astride the continental divide, the Columbia Icefield feeds rivers leading to three oceans – the Pacific, the Atlantic and the Arctic. The largest known cave system in Canada – Castleguard Cave – extends below the Columbia Icefield. No one yet knows just how far. One of the world's largest known underground rivers drains Medicine Lake, promising still larger cave systems waiting to be discovered. Some of the most famous hot springs in Canada are found here, including the Banff Hot Springs, which became the reason for establishing the first national park in Canada.

Mountain Goats

Represented by: Kluane National Park Reserve

LOCKED IN THE ICE AGE

The highest mountains in Canada, the largest non-polar icefields, the fastest, longest glaciers. This is a land in flux, a young land, a land still in the throes of creation. Volcanoes have been at work here making mountains; glaciers and rivers are carrying them away. Flowing in slow-motion, glaciers move vast amounts of pulverized rock down the valleys, sculpting the landscape. Glaciers spawn rivers opaque with silt, rivers moving mountains.

Mount Logan, Kluane National Park Reserve

THE LAND:

Mountains and glaciers – these are the essence of this region. Mount Logan, Canada's highest point at 5951 metres, towers over the massive St. Elias range. The Boundary Ranges, running north-south along the Alaska panhandle, the second major mountain system making up this region, are no less spectacular.

Lowell Glacier, Alsek River

These two mountain ranges spawn thousands of glaciers. They spill down the valleys from massive icefields. Over 2000 glaciers are found in Kluane National Park Reserve alone. These are classic valley glaciers, – some over 100 kilometres long – sinuously striped in black and white by gravel moraines.

The effects of the most recent Ice Age have not been dulled by erosion or hidden by vegetation. It is as if the ice sheets retreated yesterday. Broad U-shaped valleys, hanging valleys, cirques and other glacial landforms are evidence of their passing.

This region has some of Canada's most spectacular rivers. The Tatshenshini, the Alsek, the lower reaches of the Stikine – these and other wild, unfettered rivers provide breath-taking scenery and thrills for wilderness adventurers.

VEGETATION:

The vegetation of this region is a composite of species from the coast, the western mountains, the boreal forest, the Arctic and the northern prairies, tentatively poking up the valleys toward the glaciers and icefields. The coast forest of stately western hemlock and sitka spruce intrudes from the west; the boreal forest of sharp-pointed spruce marches up the glacier-carved valleys from the east. Alpine tundra and meadows, a complex mosaic of grasses, herbs, shrubs and dwarf trees adapted to a brief growing season and frequent snow throughout the year, prevail at higher elevations. In September, aspen brighten the mountain flanks with sheets of brilliant yellow.

Summit of Mount Logan

WILDLIFE:

This region is home to some of the continent's most spectacular wildlife – wildlife in scale with the mountains. The largest sub-species of moose in the world is found here, with bulls weighing in at over 800 kilograms. The grizzly bears are almost as big as the moose. Dall's sheep, woodland caribou, mountain goats and other large mammals abound.

STATUS OF NATIONAL PARKS:

Kluane National Park Reserve (22 015 km^2), a World Heritage Site, includes many of the natural features, wildlife and vegetation that typify this region. A wilderness area famous for its abundant grizzly bears, Dall's sheep, caribou and mountain goats, it also includes the highest mountain in Canada (Mount Logan), vast ice fields and surging glaciers. Fringing the glaciers and mountains is a narrow "green belt" ranging from coniferous and deciduous forests to alpine tundra, covering about 18 percent of the park and providing important habitat for the park reserve's abundant wildlife.

Kluane was established in 1972 when the federal government withdrew land for the national park reserve. The National Parks Act and Regulations apply but the status of the park is subject to final settlement of the Council for Yukon Indians comprehensive land claim.

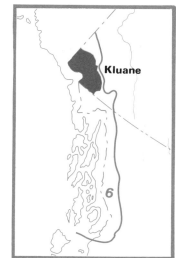

Dall's Sheep

7 Northern Interior Mountains & Plateaux

Not represented

CINDER CONES, PLATEAUX AND CANYONS

… There's the land (Have you seen it?)
It's the cussedest land that I know,
From the big, dizzy mountains that screen it,
To the deep, deathlike valleys below …

from "The Spell of the Yukon",
Robert W. Service

Grand Canyon of the Stikine

Gray Jay

Black Bear

THE LAND:

This is a large, complex region of mountains, broad plateaux, plains, basins and trenches. Glaciers and volcanoes have shaped this area extensively. The work of glaciers is present throughout, although only small icefields and glaciers exist today. Several major rivers have carved deep canyons. The "Grand Canyon of the Stikine", where the river flows for 64 kilometres between sheer lava walls 100 metres or more in height, is one of the most spectacular river canyons in Canada. The largest lakes in British Columbia are found in this region.

Spatsizi River

VEGETATION:

Boreal forest dominates the region. Black spruce, white spruce and lodgepole pine are the most common species. Sub-alpine firs stand alone or in tight groves at the tree line. Aspen and birch paint the shorelines and lower mountain sides bright yellow in September. Broad belts of alpine tundra, lush neon-green with cow parsnip and lupines or in muted pastel shades of green, grey and rust with heather and dwarf birch, are found throughout the region at higher elevations.

WILDLIFE:

Wolf

Moose, caribou, elk, Dall's and Stone's sheep, mountain goat, wolf, wolverine, black bear and grizzly bear thrive in this region. The region's many lakes and streams teem with rainbow, cutthroat and Dolly Varden trout, along with five species of salmon.

STATUS OF NATIONAL PARKS:

No national parks exist yet in this region. Four representative natural areas have been identified: **Mt. Edziza** (B.C.), **Spatsizi Plateau** (B.C.), **Kluane-Aishinik** (Yukon) and **Yukon River-Southern Ogilvies** (Yukon). Mount Edziza, the apex of the Spectrum Ranges, features well-preserved examples of recent volcanic activity, including cinder cones, calderas, lava plains, dykes and other evidence of the earth's restlessness. Much of the area is included in Mt. Edziza Provincial park.

The Spatsizi Plateau area is famous for its plentiful wildlife. Osborn caribou and Stone's sheep, two sub-species with limited ranges, find critical habitat in this area. Much of this area is included in Spatsizi Plateau Wilderness Provincial Park. Gladys Lake Ecological Reserve, the largest in the province (486 km2), is completely surrounded by the provincial park. It was established to conduct research on non-hunted big game species. No hunting or resource extraction is permitted in this area.

The Kluane-Aiskinik area adjoins Kluane National Park Reserve. This is a rugged area where alpine glaciers have carved uplands into angular mountains and U-shaped valleys. Numerous lakes, large and small, are scattered through the region. Wildlife is abundant, including many waterfowl and raptors. Among large mammals, moose are especially numerous. Most of the birds and mammals characteristic of Natural Region 7 are found here.

The Yukon River-Southern Ogilvies area includes mountains over 2500 metres high with both glaciated and unglaciated mountain landscapes. Much of this area was spared from the Pleistocene glaciers, resulting in landforms that are rarely found elsewhere in Canada. The Yukon River flows through the area; several other large rivers and lakes are found here. The wide variety of habitats supports a rich assortment of birds and mammals, including a relict Stone's sheep population. This is one of the least disturbed parts of Natural Region 7, remaining in an essentially pristine state.

Spectrum Range, B.C.

Mount Edziza

Several factors could affect national park establishment in this region. The hydro-electric power generating potential of the large rivers draining these areas — the Stikine, Stewart, and Yukon — is vast. Dams, reservoirs, transmission line rights-of-way and access roads would detract from the desirability of these areas for national park purposes. Big-game hunting and guiding is an important recreational and economic activity in much of the region. Forestry is increasing in the region, particularly in the lower Stikine Valley. Much of the region has mineral claims on it, and mines are under development in the Spatsizi Plateau area south of the provincial park.

Much of the British Columbia portion of the region is covered by several overlapping comprehensive land claims. The Association of United Tahltans comprehensive land claim covers the largest portion. The Council of Yukon Indians comprehensive land claim covers the portion of the natural region in the Yukon Territory.

Establishment of a national park in this natural region will require an agreement with the Government of British Columbia or the Yukon Territorial Government and the co-operation of the native people.

The following table summarizes the status of system planning for each step toward establishing a new national park in this natural region.

Steps in the Park Establishment Process	Status
Representative Natural Areas Identified:	done
Potential Park Area Selected:	0
Park Feasibility Assessed:	0
Park Agreement Signed:	0
Scheduled Under the National Parks Act:	0

Yukon River – Southern Ogilvies area

LIMESTONE FANTASIES

A complex land of magnificent beauty on a staggering scale. Boiling rivers sluicing through canyon walls that soar over a thousand metres upwards. Broad treeless plateaux washed in shades of red by dwarf birch. Limestone fantasy-landscapes of sinkholes, pinnacles, rock bridges and stalactite-studded caves leading "god knows where".

Virginia Falls, Nahanni National Park Reserve

THE LAND:

This is a limestone land of mountains and broad plateaux. The wide sweeping valleys of the Mackenzie and Liard rivers cut through this region. Rivers slice through the extensive high plateaux and mountains, carving deep canyons. Those of the South Nahanni River are the best known, but similar breathtaking canyons are found along other rivers in this region. Some of the most spectacular karst formations in the world are found in this region.

South Nahanni River, Third Canyon

VEGETATION:

Dense boreal forests of white and black spruce, with stands of jack- pine or lodgepole pine, cover the rolling uplands and terraces above the Mackenzie and Liard river valleys. Open boreal forests, interspersed with tundra covered by dwarf birch or grasses cloak the mountain flanks and high plateaux. Extensive areas of alpine tundra are found throughout this region.

WILDLIFE:

Large mammals include grizzly bear, black bear, woodland caribou, Dall's sheep, mountain goat, moose, wolf, lynx and many more. Wood bison have been recently re-established in the Liard Valley. The rare trumpeter swan breeds in

Golden Eagle

this region. Because of the diversity of habitats – from spruce forests to alpine tundra – both arctic and temperate species thrive here.

STATUS OF NATIONAL PARKS:

Nahanni National Park Reserve (4766 km²) represents this natural region. One of Canada's great wild rivers, the South Nahanni, rushes through this World Heritage Site. Some of the deepest river canyons in the world, spectacular mountains, bizarre karstlands, and a wealth of wildlife give this park its marvellous and unique character. Virginia Falls, more than twice the height of Niagara, is the best-known feature of the park. Nahanni includes portions of the habitats of significant wildlife species such as Dall's sheep, black and grizzly bear, wolf, golden eagle, peregrine falcon and trumpeter swan.

Proclaimed in 1976, Nahanni is scheduled as a National Park Reserve under the National Parks Act. Native land claims must be resolved before Nahanni can be proclaimed as a national park. Expansion of present boundaries will be considered in the future to improve natural theme representation and to ensure the ecological integrity of the park reserve. For example, important Dall's sheep habitat is currently excluded from the park reserve. Consultations will focus on portions of the Nahanni Karst, Tlogotsho Plateau and Ragged Range areas

Canoeing the South Nahanni, a Canadian Heritage River

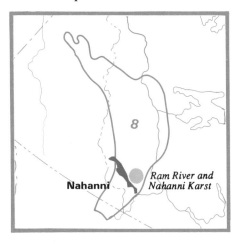

8

Nahanni

Ram River and Nahanni Karst

9 Northern Yukon

Represented by: Northern Yukon National Park (part)

COUNTRY OF THE CARIBOU

A land richer in wildlife, in variety of landscape and vegetation, and in archaeological value than any other in the Canadian Arctic. Here high mountains, spruce forests, tundra, wide 'flats' of lakes and ponds, majestic valleys ... come together to form the living fabric of the arctic wilderness.

Dr. George Calef
Wildlife Biologist,
Canadian Wildlife Service

Caribou

THE LAND:

Walking from north to south, the Northern Yukon divides into three landscapes: the rounded Richardson and British Mountains, the vast interior plains of the Old Crow Flats and the rolling Ogilvie Mountains. The Flats are covered with hundreds of rectangular lakes and meandering streams and rivers – a jigsaw water-maze.

Most of this region was bypassed by the Pleistocene glaciers. Vast sweeping pediments smooth the river valleys and isolated hills of frost-shattered rocks called tors, among other testimonials to the absence of glaciation, give the region a unique appearance.

Many palaeontological and archaeological sites have been found in this region. These include some of the best-preserved assemblages of

Pleistocene fauna and what is possibly the oldest human remains yet discovered in the western hemisphere.

VEGETATION:

Tundra blankets much of the region – alpine, moist or wet. In the mountains and foothills, alpine tundra patterns the slopes in patches and stripes.

Margaret Lake, Northern Yukon

Lichens and plants that grow as cushions or mats such as mountain avens, alpine bearberry, moss campion, woolly lousewort and purple saxifrage predominate. At lower elevations, moist tundra colours the land in the rich shades of golf greens. Cottongrass, the dominant plant, forms tussocks, making walking an ankle-twisting agony and quickly dispelling any further comparisons to golf greens. A dense, waist-high jungle of willows grows along the rivers.

The interior plain supports open stands of stunted white or black spruce, interspersed with patches of tundra and rock barrens. The most northerly tongue of forest (white spruce) in Canada is found in this region along the valley of the Firth River.

WILDLIFE:

The Porcupine Caribou Herd, one of the largest remaining ungulate herds in the world (estimated at 165,000 animals) wanders throughout this region and into Alaska. Moose are abundant in the forests of the Old Crow Flats and muskoxen have been reintroduced on the open tundra. All three species of bears – grizzly, black and polar – inhabit this region. One of the largest and most concentrated populations of grizzly bears left in the world is found here. Other wildlife includes arctic fox, arctic ground squirrel, arctic hare, lynx,

wolf, wolverine and muskrat. The Old Crow Flats is renowned for its abundance of muskrats. Although only four species of birds remain here throughout the year (the raven, willow ptarmigan and a few hardy gyrfalcons and snowy owls), the richness of the bird life in summer is staggering. Tundra swans, Canada geese and other waterfowl nest in the Old Crow Flats, one of the world's most important waterfowl habitats. The chorus arising from the tundra on a spring morning is as unforgettable as the silence of the tundra on a still winter night.

STATUS OF NATIONAL PARKS:

Northern Yukon National Park (10 168 km²), a small portion of which also extends into Natural Region 10, partly represents this region's natural features. High mountains, broad river valleys, endless tundra and the Arctic seacoast come together here to create a wilderness paradise. The portion of the park in Natural Region 9 includes

Old Crow Flats

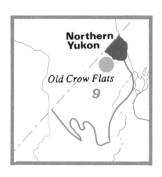

part of the British Mountains, the only extensive non-glaciated mountain range in Canada. These are rounded treeless mountains cut by smooth sweeping river valleys. The tree line – the limit beyond which trees do not grow higher than two metres - runs through this section of the park, which also harbours Canada's most northerly populations of moose and Dall's sheep.

Northern Yukon National Park was established in 1984 through agreement between the Inuvialuit of the Western Arctic and the Government of Canada. This is Canada's first national park established through a native land claim settlement. The agreement provided for the creation of a

Firth River

national park in which aboriginal harvesting rights and the wilderness character of the area are guaranteed. Local native people share the responsibility for park management.

A portion of the **Old Crow Flats** to the south of the park was part of the original proposal, and the establishment of a separate national park on the Flats is being pursued through settlement of the Council for Yukon Indians comprehensive land

claim. The creation of a national park on the Old Crow Flats would round out natural theme representation for this region. The important conservation values of Northern Yukon, including the Old Crow Flats, have long been recognized. Much of the area is designated a Ramsar site, a wetland of international importance. Since 1970, a moratorium has been placed on oil and gas exploration in the area, and in 1978, following the report of the Berger Commission on the Mackenzie Valley pipeline proposal, the lands were withdrawn under the Territorial Lands Act for conservation purposes. Speculation about possible oil and natural gas reserves in this area is a factor that could affect the establishment of a national park on the Old Crow Flats. The people of Old Crow have indicated support for the proposed park subject to the successful negotiation of their comprehensive land claim.

Steps in the Park Establishment Process	Status
Additional Natural Area Identified:	done (Old Crow Flats)
Potential Park Area Selected:	done
Park Feasibility Assessed:	in progress
Park Agreement Signed:	0
Scheduled Under the National Parks Act:	0

10 Mackenzie Delta

Represented by: Northern Yukon National Park

PINGOS AND PERMAFROST

A spongy world of pingos and permafrost, of stunted spruce forests and treeless tundra, of more water than land. A maze of shifting channels, shallow lakes and ephemeral islands. A land, too, where the traditional and the modern exist side by side.

Pingo

Mackenzie Delta

THE LAND:

Natural Region 10 comprises three distinct areas — the delta of the present Mackenzie River, remnants of earlier deltas to the northeast, and the Yukon Coastal Plain to the west. The coastal plain, about 20 kilometres wide, slopes gently to the Beaufort Sea. Permafrost is a dominant factor in this region, influencing vegetation and landforms.

The present delta, the largest river delta in Canada, is as flat as the sea. It is a tracery of islands and lakes, a labyrinth of channels and oxbows. Scores of pingos (cone-shaped hills with a core of ice) provide the only relief in this flat land. Here is found the highest concentration of pingos in the world. The tallest, Ibyuk Hill, is 40 metres high. Patterned or polygonal ground, like the pattern of cracks seen on newly dried mud on a giant scale, is a major feature of this region.

VEGETATION:

Two types of vegetation dominate. Along the Beaufort Sea is the Low Arctic or tundra zone; inland and southward is forest-tundra.

The Low Arctic vegetation is typified by dwarf shrubs, sedges and herbs. On well-drained sites, woody species such as dwarf birch, willow, Labrador tea, alder and various species of the blueberry clan are typical; on wet sites, sedges and willows dominate.

The forest-tundra zone, as its name implies, is a mixture of trees and tundra. Here, open stands of stunted black spruce, white spruce and tamarack grow over a ground cover of dwarf tundra vegetation. These are the most northerly trees in Canada. The spruce here are commonly about three metres in height and 250 years old.

WILDLIFE:

The juxtaposition of tundra and forest in this region provides for a variety of wildlife not often seen this far north. The tundra provides important summer range and calving grounds for caribou; the forest-tundra zone provides critical winter range. Barren-ground grizzlies and black bears reach the northern limit of their range here. Red fox and arctic fox, wolves, muskrat, beaver, lemming, rock ptarmigan, spruce grouse and raven are characteristic wildlife. The

Northern Yukon National Park Reserve

delta is a critical staging and nesting area for shorebirds and waterfowl. Hundreds of thousands of snow geese stop at the outer delta islands and on the coastal plain each fall to accumulate fat for the long migration south, covering the land like a dusting of snow. Beluga whales congregate offshore. Farther out to sea in the Arctic Ocean, is an important migration route and feeding area for the rare bowhead whale.

completely treeless, is typical of the Yukon Coastal Plain portion of the natural region. It is dominated by the massive fan deltas of the Firth and Malcolm rivers draining north from the British Mountains and provides critical habitat for a variety of wildlife including polar bear, muskox, wolverine, golden eagle, peregrine falcon, gyrfalcon, snow goose and arctic char. The Canadian portion of the calving ground of the Porcupine Caribou Herd lies within this portion of the park.

Expansion of the park east to include the entire Babbage River watershed will be pursued to improve representation of this natural region.

Details on park establishment are described under National Region 9.

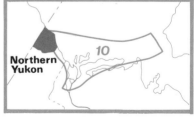

Belugas

STATUS OF NATIONAL PARKS:

About 2400 square kilometres of the northernmost part of **Northern Yukon National Park** extends into the coastal plain portion of the MacKenzie Delta Natural Region, protecting about 6 percent of the total region. This area of the park, flat and

11 Northern Boreal Plains

Represented by: Wood Buffalo National Park

Whooping Crane

WHOOPING CRANES AND BOREAL PLAINS

A vast wild plain spread with bogs, forests, meandering streams and spongy muskeg that has changed little since long before the days of the fur traders. Some of Canada's largest rivers and lakes are found in this region.

THE LAND:

What makes this region stand out is that nothing in it does – at least in terms of topography. Lowlands, plains and plateaux, underlain by horizontal beds of sedimentary rock, give this region its typical subdued relief.

What does make this region stand out are the two huge lakes, Great Bear and Great Slave, on its eastern edge and Canada's largest river, the Mackenzie. Major tributaries of the Mackenzie – the Liard, Peace, Slave – and a network of smaller rivers and streams shape the character of this region with broad floodplains crisscrossed with meandering channels and oxbow lakes.

VEGETATION:

Although this region covers a vast range of latitude, spruce prevails. In its northern reaches, open spruce forests with an understory of grey-green lichens provide winter range for caribou. Milder sites support dense forests of spruce mixed with balsam poplar, birch and aspen. In poorly drained sites, forests of black spruce and tamarack prevail – their shallow root systems spread wide in the thin layer of soggy soil. Vast treeless areas cover large parts of the region.

WILDLIFE:

The wildlife of this region is remarkable for its impermanence. Vast numbers of migratory birds take advantage of the super-abundance of food – especially insects – in the brief summer. But the long, bitterly cold winters make this region a harsh environment for year-round residents. These include the muskrat, beaver, wolf, coyote, red fox, black and grizzly bear, lynx, moose, caribou and, of course, the wood bison.

Wood Buffalo National Park

STATUS OF NATIONAL PARKS:

Wood Buffalo National Park (44 807 km²) represents this region. Small portions of the park also extend into Natural Regions 12 and 17. A World Heritage Site and home to the world's largest bison herd and the only known nesting site of the whooping crane, this is Canada's largest national park; it is also one of the largest in the world. This vast wilderness of bogs, forests, meandering streams, huge silty rivers and great tracts of spongy muskeg has changed little since prehistoric times. The sprawling Peace-Athabasca Delta, one of the world's largest inland deltas and a Ramsar site (a wetland habitat of global significance), is encompassed by the park. It is also one of the world's most impressive wildlife areas. Huge flocks of geese, swans, ducks and other water birds funnel through here each spring on their northward migration. Millions stay to nest.

Wood Bison

Wood Buffalo National Park was established in 1922 by federal Order-in-Council under the Dominion Forest Reserves and Parks Act to preserve the habitat of the wood bison. Since that time, local native people have continued to hunt, trap and fish within the park, making this the only park in Canada with a long-standing tradition of Native subsistence use. With the settlement of the Fort Chipewyan Cree land claim, mechanisms were set up for native people to participate in management decisions and to assume more responsibility for long-term stewardship of the land. The Cree claim settlement is the first in a series of native land claims that will affect the park, the largest of which is the Dene-Métis claim covering the portion of the park that lies in the Northwest Territories.

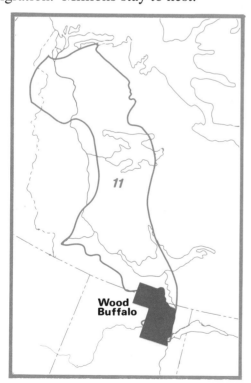
Wood Buffalo

12 Southern Boreal Plains & Plateaux

Represented by: Wood Buffalo National Park (8% of total area of park);
Riding Mountain National Park; Elk Island National Park; Prince Albert National Park

Prince Albert National Park

A REGION OF TRANSITION

A region of transition, from the dry, treeless prairies to the moist boreal forest, from intensely man-altered landscapes to pristine wilderness. Within this region are some of the most endangered habitats in Canada.

Riding Mountain National Park

THE LAND:

The topography of this region is a gentle blend of plains and plateaux, with a few widely scattered groups of low hills and wide river valleys. To the north is the Alberta Plateau, with hills reaching heights of about 200 metres. To the south are smooth plains. The underlying soft sedimentary bedrock has influenced the regular relief found in this region. Subsequent glaciation has modified the landscape, leaving rolling moraines on the uplands and fine-grained lacustrine deposits in lowland areas.

VEGETATION:

Although this region is one of continuous transition from prairie through deciduous forest to boreal forest, three distinctive vegetation zones are recognized. In the south, aspen parkland, a mosaic of trembling aspen groves and rough fescue grasslands, is the prevalent vegetation. This combination of communities forms a distinctive Canadian habitat that is unique in the world. Bordering the aspen parkland is a zone of mixedwood forest containing various combinations of coniferous species (white spruce

Beaver, re-introduced to Elk Island National Park

and balsam fir) and deciduous species (white birch, trembling aspen, balsam poplar). At the extreme north end of this natural region, seemingly endless stretches of black spruce muskeg dominate much of the flat, poorly drained land.

WILDLIFE:

The aspen parkland is extremely productive wildlife habitat. White-tailed deer, coyotes, snowshoe hares and ground squirrels are conspicuous mammals. The numerous potholes in this zone provide for the highest density of breeding dabbling ducks in North America, particularly mallards, shovellers and pintails. In the past, vast herds of bison ranged into this zone.

The northern forest zones, though not as rich in wildlife as the aspen parkland, are characterized by moose, black bear, muskrat, beaver, lynx, wolverine and wolf. Wood bison are resident in the extreme northern portions of this region. Some of the more notable migrants to the northern most reaches of this region include the whooping crane, white pelican and sandhill crane.

STATUS OF NATIONAL PARKS:

Four national parks represent this natural region: **Elk Island** (194 km^2), **Riding Mountain** (2,976 km^2), **Prince Albert** (3,875 km^2) and **Wood Buffalo** (3,584 km^2 or 8% of the total area of the park).

Elk Island is a fenced wildlife sanctuary of forested hills and rolling meadows surrounded by grain fields and pastures in the aspen parkland zone of this natural region. Wandering herds of plains bison and elk can be seen from scenic parkways and trails winding around lakes and beaver ponds. Public interest in the conservation of rapidly dwindling wildlife led to the establishment of Elk Island National Park in 1913.

Like Elk Island, Riding Mountain is an island of forest rising out of a sea of farmland. The park includes a diversity of landscapes – evergreen and hardwood forests, rolling hills, valleys, lakes and streams. A plateau in the centre of North America, the park is a crossroads where prairie, boreal and deciduous life zones mingle. The park is the core protected area of Riding Mountain Biosphere Reserve. The park was set aside by the federal government in 1929 as part of the Riding Mountain Forest Reserve.

Bounded on the south by farmland, Prince Albert exhibits the variety of vegetation and landscapes

Elk Island National Park

that typifies this region. Pockets of aspen parklands and fescue prairies in the south of the park blend with mixedwood forests and boreal forests in the park's northern reaches. A network of lakes and rivers makes this a popular park for canoeists. For seven years, from 1931 to 1938, Grey Owl, the controversial conservationist, lived on the shore of Ajawaan Lake in the park. The park was established in 1927 by the federal government to "preserve in perpetuity a portion of

Riding Mountain National Park

the primitive forest and lake country of Northern Saskatchewan and to provide for the people of Saskatchewan ... a great recreational area."

A description of Wood Buffalo National Park is included under Natural Region 11.

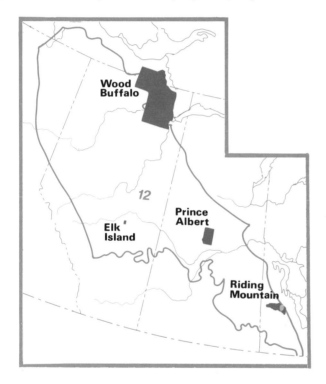

13 Prairie Grasslands

Represented by: Grasslands National Park

Grasslands National Park

PRONGHORNS AND PRAIRIE DOGS

This natural region is often referred to in the past tense, in terms of what once was. It was once an ocean of grass, broken by wide wooded valleys and forest-clad hills. It was once Canada's richest wildlife region, reminiscent of the savannah country of East Africa. But we will never really know what it was like. Only the wind remains unchanged, blowing unceasingly across the sweeping plains.

THE LAND:

A vast tilted plain, the land rises gently until it ends abruptly at the foothills of the Rockies. The monotonous flatness is interrupted by weirdly eroded badlands, sand dunes, coulees, rocky canyons, potholes, hills and sweeping river valleys. This region rests on a thick mantle of rich, black soil that is cool and moist to the touch – some of the most fertile in the country. Within the fertile grasslands is "Palliser's Triangle", semiarid country considered unsuitable for agriculture or stock raising in the opinion of John Palliser, leader of a scientific expedition along the American boundary in 1857-1860.

Prairie Crocus

VEGETATION:

Speargrass, wheatgrass, blue grama, rough fescue, bluebunch fescue, red fescue, needlegrass, little blue-stem — grass is the single characteristic common to the mosaic of habitats making up this region. Mixed prairie, dominated by speargrasses and wheatgrasses, is the most extensive grassland type in this region. Mixed

Burrowing Owl

Prairie, as its name implies, includes both tall and short grasses. Blue grama, a drought-resistant short grass, is important in dry sites.

River valleys and old drainage channels, important routes for the invasion of plant species that survived the last glaciation beyond the edge of the ice sheet, harbour a rich variety of trees and shrubs: oaks, American elm, cottonwood, Manitoba maple, and green ash, among others. Shallow depressions, some of which are periodically flooded, harbour communities of salt-resistant species, such as alkali grass and wild barley. The thousands of sloughs that characterize this region, ranging in area from a few square metres to several hectares, are dominated by tall sedges and grasses.

WILDLIFE:

It is difficult to imagine the richness of the wildlife of this natural region in pre-settlement days. Herds of bison so vast that they took days to pass, along with untold numbers of pronghorn antelope, mule deer, white-tailed deer and elk, roamed this wilderness of grass stalked by the prairie grizzly, prairie wolf, cougar and other predators.

13
Grasslands

Today only remnants of this rich fauna remain in the most remote and driest corners of the region. Here, species endemic to the prairies, such as the pronghorn antelope, black-tailed prairie dog and plains pocket gopher, can still be found. The black-footed ferret and greater prairie chicken once lived here, but are believed to have been extirpated.

Waterfowl nest in the potholes that dimple this region, earning it the title "The Duck Factory of North America". The open grasslands still provide habitat for such unique prairie species as the sage grouse and sharp-tailed grouse, along with introduced species such as the ring-necked pheasant and the Hungarian partridge.

Several interesting species of reptiles and amphibians are restricted in Canada to this region: the prairie rattlesnake, the eastern short-horned lizard, the plains spadefoot toad, and the great plains toad, among others.

STATUS OF NATIONAL PARKS:

This region will be represented by **Grasslands National Park**. In the dry hills, badlands and eroded river valleys, a diversity of wildlife, including pronghorns, rattlesnakes and the only remaining black-tailed prairie dog colonies in Canada, can still be found in this corner of the prairies. A 1981 agreement between the Government of Canada and the Government of Saskatchewan, revised in 1988, provides for the establishment of the park encompassing 906 square kilometres. Certain watercourses will remain under the control of the province but will be managed consistent with policies and regulations governing national parks. The park will be proclaimed under the National Parks Act once sufficient lands have been acquired.

Long Point

FLAT PLAINS AND WATER

A diversity of landscapes and life – chequerboard wheat fields growing on ancient endless lakebeds, river valleys burnished copper in fall with burr oak, buttery-green rolling meadows, sweeping sand beaches, broad shallow lakes and some of the most productive freshwater marshes in North America.

THE LAND:

This region is more than one-half covered by water – huge, shallow lakes, potholes, ponds and vast cattail marshes. These are the legacy of an immense glacial lake, Lake Aggasiz, that once covered most of the area. Today, ridges of sand and gravel marking ancient beaches and shorelines separate the lakes and meander gracefully across the land. Underlain by flat beds of sedimentary rock, the level topography of this region is a product of the last glaciation – scoured by ice and smoothed by the deposition of sediments from ancient glacial meltwater lakes.

VEGETATION:

This region supports a diversity of vegetation, from spruce forest to prairie. The northern two-thirds of the region is a wilderness of spruce: white spruce mixed with birch and aspen on the better drained sites; black spruce mixed with tamarack on the wetter sites. A groveland dominated by burr-oak and aspen mixed with open prairie forms a broad transition to the true tall-grass prairie of the southern extremities of the region. A small remnant of tall-grass prairie, one of the few left in existence, is located in the City of Winnipeg and managed as the Living Prairie Museum. Vast areas of the region are covered by cattail marshes.

Coyote

WILDLIFE:

The spruce forests are typified by moose, black bear and sharp-tailed grouse, while the burr-oak groves and prairies are frequented by wildlife more typical of the prairies – white-tailed deer, coyote, and Franklin's and thirteen-lined ground squirrels. Bison, mule deer, pronghorn antelope, elk and wolf thrived here in the recent past.

The extensive marshes of this region are critical nesting and staging areas for a myriad of birds, especially waterfowl. Delta Marsh, North America's largest fresh-water marsh, remains in a relatively undisturbed state. Winter denning sites

Eared Grebe

for thousands of garter snakes are found along the limestone outcrops on the west side of Lake Winnipeg.

The shallow lakes covering much of this region support an abundance and diversity of fish species, as well as a thriving commercial and sport fishing industry. Over 70 species have been recorded, with pike, whitefish, sauger and walleye the most important commercial species.

STATUS OF NATIONAL PARKS:

No national parks exist yet in this region. Three representative natural areas have been identified, at **Little Limestone Lake, Long Point and Hecla**. Due to recent disturbances, these sites need to be re-evaluated. Long Point, bordering on

Hecla Island

Lake Winnipeg, is noted for its mature white cedar forests. It provides habitat for woodland caribou, moose, elk, migrating raptors, great grey owls, waterfowl, shorebirds and an abundance and diversity of fish. Over 1600 hectares of this site are protected as an ecological reserve. Little Limestone Lake is noted for its varied landforms (flood plains, sinkholes, glacial till) and diverse vegetation, including fens, bogs and boreal forest. The limestone bedrock is responsible for the remarkable clarity and emerald colour in several lakes. Hecla, located on the transition from Canadian Shield to the Manitoba Lowlands and from Aspen Oak to spruce forest, displays a wonderful diversity of life and landscapes in a small area. It is noted for its colonies of great blue herons, terns, grebes and gulls, as well as abundant moose and wolves. Much of this area is under provincial jurisdication as Hecla Island Provincial Park.

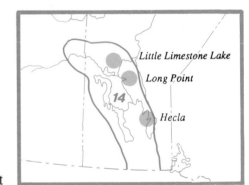

The establishment of a national park in this natural region will require an agreement with the Government of Manitoba.

The following table summarizes the status of system planning for each step towards establishing a new national park in this natural region.

Steps in the Park Establishment Process	Status
Representative Natural Areas Identified:	done
Potential Park Area Selected:	0
Park Feasibility Assessed:	0
Park Agreement Signed:	0
Scheduled Under the National Parks Act:	0

15 Tundra Hills

Not represented

Wilberforce Falls

BREAKFAST WITH CARIBOU, LUNCH WITH MUSKOXEN

The coast consists of precipitous banks ... the shale was in a state of ignition in many places and the hot sulphureous airs from the land were strongly contrasted with the cold sea-breezes ... the baked clays of yellow, brown, white and red colours caused the place to resemble a brick field or pottery.

J. Richardson, 1826,
describing the "Smoking Hills".

THE LAND:

The western part of this region is underlain by sedimentary bedrock in undisturbed horizontal layers creating a landscape of plains, patterned ground and pingos. The eastern part of the region is part of the ancient Canadian Shield. Here the topography is rugged and hilly, with many lakes, large and small. The ice sheets have added the final touches to the landscape — eskers, drumlins, deposits of glacial till and other glacial features. Step-like series of raised cobble beaches and marine clay deposits more than 60 metres above sea level are a testimonial to the combination of higher sea levels in post-glacial times and the re-bounding of the land after being released from the weight of the glaciers. The rivers have cut deep gorges and canyons through the sedimentary bedrock. These have been compared to the canyons of the southwest United States. Wilberforce Falls on the Hood River is one of the most spectacular waterfalls in Canada.

Perhaps the most remarkable feature of this region is the "smoking hills", a site of slow-burning

Smoking Hills

– 43 –

bituminous coal. In this landscape, which resembles paintings of Hell, sulphur fumes have killed off the vegetation, and smoke billows from the cracks in the ash-covered ground.

VEGETATION:

More than 95 percent of this region is tundra — rock barrens where mountain avens and purple saxifrage grow in dense mats; polar deserts where only lichens can thrive; verdant wet sedge meadows; dense carpets of willows, dwarf birch and heath vegetation. An undulating band of stunted, creeping spruce trees interspersed among the heaths and other typical tundra species extends into this region along river valleys, marking the northerly limit of tree growth.

WILDLIFE:

The wildlife of this region features few resident species and many summer migrants. This reflects the difference in the availability of food between the continuous summer sunshine and the long, dark winter.

Willow Ptarmigan

Two major caribou herds, the Bluenose Herd and the Bathurst Herd, migrate throughout this region. Together they account for up to 250,000 animals, among the largest caribou herds in Canada. Native peoples in the region still depend on the caribou as they have for thousands of years. There are also significant populations of muskox in the region that are recovering from over-hunting early in the 20th century.

The only remaining nesting ground for the Eskimo curlew, perhaps the rarest bird in Canada, is in this region. In the 1800s it existed in huge flocks, but by 1900 it was hovering on the brink of extinction, another victim of over-hunting.

STATUS OF NATIONAL PARKS:

In 1978, Bathurst Inlet was proposed as a national park. However, when geological studies showed that the area has high mineral potential, work on the proposal was suspended. The Canadian Parks Service is currently working to establish a national park in the **Bluenose Lake** area. In 1989, the Inuvialuit expressed strong interest in establishing a national park in this area to protect the Bluenose caribou herd's calving grounds. Also included within the park study area are such features as the spectacular Hornaday River Canyon, the dissected Melville Hills and abundant wildlife, including caribou, muskox, grizzly bear and wolf. Consultations with local residents and native groups to ascertain support for a national park, which began in 1989, are ongoing. Studies are being undertaken to collect detailed information on past

Hornaday River

Anderson River

and present land use, cultural resources, wildlife, and vegetation, as well as to assess mineral potential. Land ownership is an important issue that may affect park establishment. The study area includes Inuvialuit lands along the Arctic coast. As well, about 40 percent of the proposed park lies within the Tungavik Federation of Nunavut (TFN) land-claim area.

Establishment of a national park in the Bluenose Lake area will require the support and co-operation of the residents of Paulatuk and Coppermine, the Inuvialuit, the Tungavik Federation of Nunavut and the Government of the Northwest Territories. The following table summarizes the status of system planning for each step towards establishing a new national park in this natural region.

Bluenose Lake area

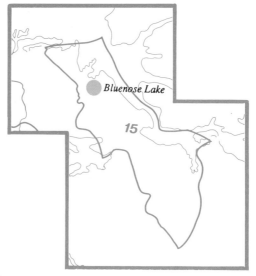

Steps in the Park Establishment Process	Status
Representative Natural Areas Identified:	done
Potential Park Area Selected:	done
Park Feasibility Assessed:	in progress
Park Agreement Signed:	0
Scheduled Under the National Parks Act:	0

16 Central Tundra

Not represented

Esker

WHERE TIME AND LIGHT STAND STILL

Glorious it is to see,
The caribou flocking down from the forests,
Spreading out over plains of white,
… Glorious it is to see,
The great musk oxen,
Gathering in herds...Glorious to see

Traditional Inuit song recorded in the
Report of the Fifth Thule Expedition, 1921-24

THE LAND:

Tundra superimposed on the Canadian Shield is the characteristic that makes this region stand out. The landscape is remarkably uniform – an endless series of low ridges, broken by a myriad of jigsaw-puzzle lakes and broad rivers. Evidence of Pleistocene glaciers is found throughout the region. Eskers wind across the land. Old beaches and deposits of marine clay over 200 metres above present sea level show that the entire region must have been awash in gigantic lakes and rivers at the melting of the last great ice sheets.

This region is wilderness unbroken, save for a few communities. However, evidence of human use is found throughout the region – inukshuks (stone markers), food caches, and hunters' blinds, pits and campsites that have been used for centuries.

VEGETATION:

The entire region is characterized by an almost continuous cover of low tundra vegetation consisting of dwarf birch, willow, Labrador tea, dryas, and various species of the blueberry clan. A broken fringe of boreal forest clings to sheltered river valleys.

Muskox

WILDLIFE:

Here is the world of the Pleistocene, or as close as one can get to it today – a world where the wildlife remains in its primeval state. Here you can watch white wolves hunting among vast herds of caribou, barren-ground grizzlies patrolling their riverbank domains and polar bears cruising the coast of Hudson Bay. In the fastness of the Thelon Game Sanctuary, muskox bulls stare, stiff-legged, at human intruders. Untold numbers of Canada geese, snow geese, tundra swans and other waterfowl nest and moult in the Queen Maud Gulf Migratory Bird Sanctuary, a Ramsar site (wetland of international importance) and the largest

largest protected area in Canada (62 000 km²). Overhead, golden eagles, bald eagles, gyrfalcons, peregrine falcons, rough-legged hawks and other birds of prey soar.

Hanbury River

STATUS OF NATIONAL PARKS:

No national parks have yet been established in this natural region. A national park in the **Wager Bay** area has been proposed since 1978. Wager Bay, a veritable inland sea, extends more than 150 kilometres inland from Hudson Bay. Glacier-polished islands and shorelines, colourful cliffs and tidal flats backed by rolling tundra give this area its special appeal. A reversing falls at the indland end of Wager Bay and a polynya (an area of the sea that never freezes) at its mouth are features of special interest.

The wildlife that has attracted hunters to this area since ancient times still abounds. Polar bears congregate here in summer and can regularly be seen along the shore; peregrine falcons and gyrfalcons nest on the cliffs; caribou roam the tundra hills. Tent rings and disused meat caches are found along the shoreline, indicating that the area has long been a favoured hunting ground. Residents from Repulse Bay and from as far away as Chesterfield Inlet, Rankin Inlet and Coral Harbour still travel to the area to hunt for seals and caribou and to fish for arctic char.

Wager Bay remains almost completely untouched. There are no permanent inhabitants, although a commercial lodge was recently built that caters primarily to naturalists. The terms of settlement of the Tungavik Federation of Nunavut comprehensive land claim, which covers the entire

Caribou, Thelon Game Sanctuary

natural region, could affect park establishment. Local support for a national park must also be ascertained.

The next step in the park establishment process will be discussions with local people to explore the idea of a national park in the context of land-use planning for the Keewatin Region and the land claim of the Inuit of the Eastern Arctic.

Establishment of a national park in the Wager Bay area will require the support and co-operation of the residents of Repulse Bay and Rankin Inlet, the Tungavik Federation of Nunavut and the Government of the Northwest Territories.

The **Thelon Game Sanctuary,** established in 1927 as an area exempt from hunting and resource extraction, is an alternative area that merits further study if the Wager Bay proposal is not successful.

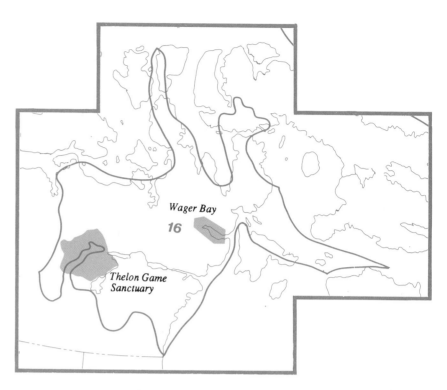

Abandoned Hudson's Bay Company Post, Wager Bay

The following table summarizes the status of system planning for each step toward establishing a new national park in this natural region.

Steps in the Park Establishment Process	Status
Representative Natural Areas Identified:	done
Potential Park Area Selected:	done
Park Feasibility Assessed:	in progress
Park Agreement Signed:	0
Scheduled Under the National Parks Act:	0

17 Northwestern Boreal Uplands

Not represented

Great Slave Lake

"LAND OF LITTLE STICKS"

Lakes, lakes, lakes innumerable...The first bay we investigated ... developed into a baffling labyrinth of small enclosures and twisting points, islands and channels, hills, knolls, promontories, and even lakelets within lakes. God help the man who gets off the route in this country! Nothing – nothing to go by ... just thousands and thousands of caribou trails.

*from the journals of P.G. Downes,
on a trip from Reindeer Lake
to Nueltin Lake in 1939*

THE LAND:

Ridge after low ridge of granite or gneiss, innumerable interlocking lakes and tumbling rivers, endless spruce forests — the edge of the Canadian Shield marks the western boundary of this region. Here the region abuts onto the great Shield-edge lakes – Great Bear, Great Slave, Athabasca, Wollaston, Reindeer, South Indian – famous for their interlocking convolutions of islands and bays.

Hoarfrost River

The continental ice sheets have left their footprints on the entire region in the form of glacier-scoured lake-filled basins and large expanses of exposed bedrock smoothed and scored by the passing glaciers. Erratics, boulders left behind by the melting of the glaciers, are sprinkled liberally over the land, and massive eskers, up to 75 metres high, slither indiscriminately across lakes and over the land for tens of kilometres. Glacial erosion and deposition have left an intricate maze of labyrinthine lakes connected by short sections of rapid-strewn rivers.

VEGETATION:

This is a region of spruce forests. In the more temperate parts of the region, the shores of the lakes and rivers are heavily treed with dense forests of black spruce, white spruce and white birch. A closed-canopy forest of spruce and jack pine, with an understory of feathermoss, lichens, blueberries and cranberries, covers the southern part of the region. Toward the north are open woodlands of black spruce spaced 5-10 metres apart and rarely reaching 15 metres in height. A mat of lichens up to 15 centimetres thick carpets the ground between the trees. On the northern fringe of the region, even more open stands of stunted black spruce and tamarack with a ground cover of dwarf tundra vegetation form a transition to the barrenlands.

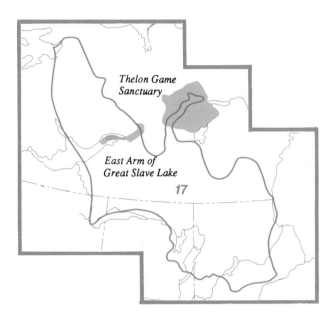

WILDLIFE:

This is a region rich in wildlife. Vast herds of caribou winter here in the spruce forests, some staying all year round. In late October, after the rutting season, the great bands of caribou mass up on the edge of the woods and spend the harshest winter months in the spruce and pine forests. The females start to work their way north again in February or March, bearing their young on the barren-grounds in June. By July, they are on the move again toward the forests.

The region has long been famous as a source of furs – beaver, muskrat, lynx, wolf, red fox, wolverine, martin, mink, otter. Moose and black bear are also abundant. Lake trout, white fish and huge northern pike thrive in the cold, nutrient-poor lakes and rivers.

STATUS OF NATIONAL PARKS:

For more than 20 years, an area known as the **East Arm of Great Slave Lake/Artillery Lake** has been considered for a national park. In 1970, 7150 square kilometres of land in this area was withdrawn under the Territorial Lands Act for national park purposes. This is a spectacular landscape – an immense archipelago of islands in Great Slave Lake, long fault-block escarpments, gorges and waterfalls, and much more.

Early negotiations stalled due to concerns raised by native peoples from the community of Snowdrift about the effects of a national park on

their traditional use of the land and on their lifestyle. Negotiations are once again continuing, under the Dene/Métis land-claim settlement process. The Minister of the Environment has promised that the park will not be established without the support of the people of Snowdrift. The support and co-operation of the Dene-Métis and the Government of the Northwest Territories are also required.

Other possible representative natural areas include Conjuror Bay on Great Bear Lake and Athabasca North Shore.

The following table summarizes the status of system planning for each step toward establishing a new national park in this natural region.

Steps in the Park Establishment Process	Status
Representative Natural Areas Identified:	done
Potential Park Areas Selected:	done
Park Feasibility Assessed:	in progress
Park Agreement Signed:	0
Scheduled Under the National Park Act :	0

18 Central Boreal Uplands

Represented by: Pukaskwa National Park

Oiseau Bay, Pukaskwa National Park

AN INFINITY OF ROCK, WATER AND WOOD

A rugged wilderness of endless spruce forests and quaking bogs, of rock-rimmed lakes and tumbling rivers teeming with walleye, pike and trout, of moose and beaver and hordes of black flies. This region is synonymous with the Canadian Shield, the quintessential Canadian landscape. The combination of rock, water and dense forest makes this region tough country to walk in. But it is a land made for the canoe.

Cascade River, Pukaskwa National Park

the glaciers that gave the land its final shape. The legacy of the glaciers can be seen everywhere – in the tortuous watersheds and the myriad lakes, ponds and bogs; in the exposed glacier-scarred bedrock; and in the moraines and drumlins hidden under the never-ending spruce forests.

One of the few anomalies in the uniformity of this region is the Athabasca Sand Dunes in northern Saskatchewan. These are the most extensive sand dunes in Canada. Open shifting dunes intermix with stabilized dunes, resulting in a unique landscape characterized by an unusual assemblage of plants, many of which are restricted to this site.

THE LAND:

This is a raw land, still healing from the effects of the Ice Age. The ancient granite and gneiss of the Canadian Shield, lying exposed or covered by a thin acidic layer of grey-brown soil, give the entire region its characteristic rugged relief. The Precambrian rock is the clay from which this landscape of rough hills was formed, but it was

VEGETATION:

White spruce, black spruce, balsam fir ... white spruce, black spruce, balsam fir ... this pattern repeats itself endlessly across the region. The forest is outstanding in its uniformity. Tamarack and jack pine, along with fast-growing deciduous species such as poplar and birch, are other important members of the forest cast. Along the southern edge of the region, white pine and red pine, sugar maple, black ash, eastern white cedar and other species from the Great Lakes-St. Lawrence forest intermix in sheltered areas and depressions in which soil has accumulated. Along the northern border, the harsh climate results in an open coniferous forest with a thick mat of lichens growing between the trees.

Beaver

Numberless bogs and fens support black spruce, Labrador tea, blueberries and their kin, bog rosemary, cloudberry and other acid-loving species.

WILDLIFE:

For many, the beaver is the symbol of this area. It was the desirability of its pelt that shaped the history of this region. For others, the loon is the symbol of the boreal forest. Other typical wildlife include the moose, wolf, snowshoe hare, spruce grouse, ruffed grouse, lynx, black bear and caribou (old-growth forests providing their critical winter range). In summer, the spruce woods ring with the calls of warblers and other migratory birds.

STATUS OF NATIONAL PARKS:

This region is represented by **Pukaskwa National Park** (1878 km^2), a rugged wilderness of rock-rimmed lakes, tumbling rivers and dense forests, bounded by the rocky headlands and sheltered cobble and sand beaches of Lake Superior. A small herd of woodland caribou, a rare species in Canada, shares the park hinterland with moose, wolf, black bear and a host of smaller creatures. Hike the challenging Coastal Trail or paddle the shore of Lake Superior to experience Pukaskwa's wild beauty.

Pukaskwa was established in 1978 pursuant to a federal-provincial agreement with the Government of Ontario. A native land claim and regulations related to traditional renewable resource harvesting must be settled for Pukaskwa National Park to be proclaimed under the National Parks Act.

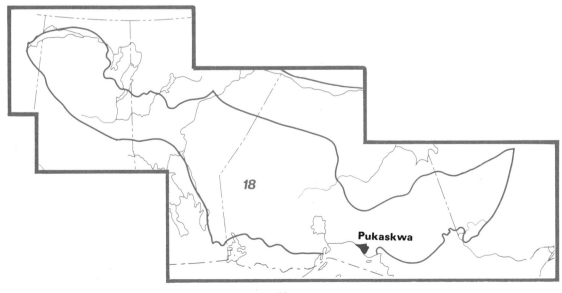

19 Great Lakes – St. Lawrence Precambrian

Represented by: St. Lawrence Islands National Park; La Mauricie National Park; Georgian Bay Islands National Park (part)

Common Loon

WHERE NORTH MEETS SOUTH

This is loon country, cottage country, famous for its dazzling autumn forests of scarlet and gold and its innumerable lakes and waterways. Like the boreal shield country to the north, this region is deeply ingrained into the image of Canada.

THE LAND:

Although this region has three separate sections, it is united by two distinctive characteristics: the mixed forest of coniferous and deciduous trees and the ancient bedrock of the southern edge of the Canadian Shield. The entire region is a transition zone, where species from the deciduous forests to the south intermingle with those of the

boreal forests to the north and, to a lesser extent, those from the western plains, the Atlantic coast and the Arctic.

Each section is remarkably similar in appearance – knobbly wooded hills incised by rivers and streams and dotted with thousands of lakes. Rivers and streams run slowly, backed up by numerous beaver dams and rocky ledges. The effects of the Ice Age are everywhere written on the land. Extensive areas of exposed bedrock are common, much of it scoured and scraped smooth by the passing of the glaciers; in other areas, glacial till or deposits left by ancient meltwater rivers soften the relief.

VEGETATION:

The three sections making up this region are covered with a mosaic of coniferous and deciduous forest that are aflame with colour each fall. The region is one of continuous transition, with many species reaching their northern or southern range limits here. Along its northern

Petawawa River, Algonquin Provincial Park

border, species common to the boreal forest – white spruce, black spruce, white birch, jack pine, balsam fir – make up a high percentage of total forest cover. In the southern portion of the region, sugar maple, American beech, basswood, white elm, red maple and other species common to the pure deciduous forests predominate. Eastern hemlock, yellow birch, white pine and red pine are found throughout the region.

WILDLIFE:

This is also a region of transition for wildlife, with

Red Fox

many species reaching their northern or southern range limits here. Wildlife typical of the boreal forest, such as moose, lynx, snowshoe hare and timber wolf are widespread, but reach their southern limits here. Chipmunk, mourning dove, cardinal and wood thrush are just a sampling of widespread species from southern forests that

Cardinal Flower

reach their northern limits here. Range limits change quickly in this region, reflecting the habitat alterations that are continuously occurring because of the effects of humans or natural fluctuations in climate, with some expanding northward and others spreading to the south. Many species have limited ranges or disjunct populations within this region – eastern hognose snake, black rat snake, eastern massasauga rattlesnake, eastern ribbon snake, southern flying squirrel, piping plover, the re-introduced wild turkey, and Blanding's turtle, among many others.

STATUS OF NATIONAL PARKS:

Three national parks represent this region: **St. Lawrence Islands** (6 km^2), **La Mauricie** (544 km^2) and **Georgian Bay Islands** (25 km^2). St. Lawrence Islands National Park, composed mainly of granite islands scattered for 80 kilometres along the St. Lawrence River, presents a remarkable diversity of flora and fauna, including many species considered rare, threatened or endangered such as the pitch pine and the black rat snake. Each island has its own particular mix of species, depending on its size, bedrock and recent history. A short walk across many islands can take you from a hardwood forest typical of areas much further south to moist shady slopes where northern species flourish.

Red Trillium

Autumn Leaves, La Mauricie National Park

The islands that make up the park were formerly Indian lands, surrendered under treaty and held in trust by the Government of Canada. By the turn of the century, many had been sold for summer homes. In 1904, local residents urged the federal government to reserve for the public nine islands designated for sale. These formed the nucleus of the park, which was formally established in 1914.

La Mauricie National Park is quintessential "Shield Country", a land of rich mixed-wood forests and over 150 lakes set into the gently rolling Laurentian Hills. Sport fishing for

speckled and lake trout and canoe tripping along the routes that crisscross the park are the best ways to experience La Mauricie's Laurentian heritage. The park was established in 1970 pursuant to a federal-provincial agreement with the Government of Quebec.

Georgian Bay Islands National Park consists of 59 islands and shoals on the east side of Georgian Bay. The park is a transition between natural regions 29 and 19. This interface results in a merging of many habitats, giving the park a great diversity of flora and fauna and many rare species. More species of reptiles and amphibians, including the eastern Massasauga rattlesnake, are found here than in any other national park.

The islands making up the park were formerly Indian lands surrendered by the Chippewa in 1856 and held in trust by the Department of Indian Affairs. By the turn of the century, the Georgian Bay region had become a popular vacation area with waterfront lands quickly being bought up. With commendable foresight, the Commissioner of National Parks, J.B. Harkin, recommended the purchase of 28 islands from the Department of Indian Affairs in 1924. The park was formally scheduled in 1929.

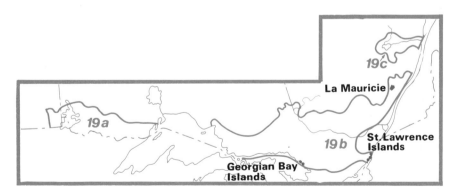

Manitou River

BALSAM, BOGS, BLACK FLIES AND BOREAL

This region at first appears monotonous in its simplicity. It is an elemental landscape – Precambrian bedrock scoured and softened by the work of glaciers, with a cold, damp climate giving the final brushstrokes – an uninterrupted cloak of gloomy boreal forest.

THE LAND:

This region is most spectacular along its eastern border, rising abruptly in bold headlands 300-600 metres from the St. Lawrence Estuary. Moving inland, the interior relief is rugged, undulating and deeply incised by large rivers tumbling downhill into the St. Lawrence. One of these, the Moisie, is famous among white-water wilderness adventurers.

The entire region is underlain by the Precambrian gneisses of the Canadian Shield. The Shield is shattered by two large meteorite craters: The Manicougan and the Malbaie. These have left distinctive marks on the normally impervious shield – a mountainous uplifted core at the centre of the strike and a circular depression marking the outer rim of the crater walls. (This feature of the Manicougan Crater has been flooded by hydro-electric power-generating dams and is easily visible on a map as a circle of lakes.)

VEGETATION:

This is a region of dark, damp and dense forests, spreading in uniform monotony along the St. Lawrence to the sea and northward to the tundra. The blanket of boreal forest is interrupted only by

Bogs near St. Lawrence River

the valley of the Saguenay, where the mixed-forest of Region 19 makes a brief appearance.

But within the monotony is variety caused by fire and topography. From the air the land is a patchwork of colour – the black evergreen forest, bright green patches of deciduous trees, and pastel hues of brown and yellow marking the bogs.

A complete cross section of the boreal ecosystem exists in this region. In the southern portions, black spruce and balsam fir dominate, with stands of white birch where logging and fires have occurred. Farther inland, the forests of spruce and fir become denser, with a uniform understory of moss. Bogs blot large areas in sinuous stripes or Rorschach-shaped blotches. Along the northern edge of the region, black-spruce forests, perpetuated by fires, take over from the balsam fir. However, in undisturbed sites, the balsam fir is the climax species. White spruce grows on well-drained sites; bogs soak up excess water in poorly drained depressions.

WILDLIFE:

Caribou, moose, black bear, wolf, lynx, snowshoe hare and other mammals typical of the boreal forest are common here. Conspicuous birds include the pileated woodpecker (Canada's largest woodpecker), ruffed grouse and black duck.

Lynx

The large rivers dropping rapidly into the Gulf of St. Lawrence provide important spawning grounds for Atlantic salmon.

This region provides ideal conditions for two other creatures: the black fly and the spruce budworm. The region has plenty of cold, shallow swift-flowing streams, ideal nurseries for black flies. The spruce budworm, despite its name, prefers to feed on balsam fir, of which there are plenty in this region. The numbers of this species regularly reach epidemic proportions.

STATUS OF NATIONAL PARKS:

No national parks exist yet in this region. A regional study to identify representative natural areas must now be completed. Factors that could affect new park establishment include widespread logging and the hydroelectric power potential of this natural region's rivers. Establishment of a national park in this natural region will require an agreement with the Government of Quebec and the resolution of the Conseil Attikamek-Montagnais, whose comprehensive land claim affects the area.

The following table summarizes the status of system planning for each step toward establishing a new national park in this natural region.

Steps in the Park Establishment Process	Status
Representative Natural Areas Identified:	0
Potential Park Area Selected:	0
Park Feasibility Assessed:	0
Park Agreement Signed:	0
Scheduled Under the National Parks Act:	0

Jewel Lake, Mealy Mountains

SEA OF SPRUCE

"The land should not be called the New land, being composed of stones and horrible rugged rocks ... I am rather inclined to believe that this is the land god gave to Cain".

Jacques Cartier, 1534

THE LAND:

This is the easternmost extension of the Canadian Shield. Along the southern edge of the region, the coastline resembles the edge of an unfinished jigsaw puzzle, with bold, jutting headlands, bays and a frieze of islands. From the Strait of Belle Isle, the land rises abruptly 200-400 metres to forested slopes dissected by swift rivers. Inland is a rolling plateau strewn with bogs and amoeboid

Mealy Mountains area

lakes woven together by a tracery of rivers full of rapids. Meandering eskers and lines of boulders crisscross the plateau.

The cold Labrador Current brings Arctic waters, chilling the land. Icebergs are often seen along the coast, earning it the nickname "Iceberg Alley". Fog is frequent, and intense storms regularly buffet this region.

Several interesting historical sites are found in this area. At Red Bay, site of a Basque whaling station in the fifteenth century, the oldest shipwreck north of the Caribbean has been uncovered along with numerous artefacts. Moravian missions established in 1782 and 1830 at Hopedale and Hebron have been designated as national historic sites. The original building at Hopedale is still standing, the oldest frame structure in eastern Canada.

VEGETATION:

The vegetation of this region is a continuous transition from boreal forest to arctic tundra. Along the exposed southeastern coast and interior uplands, the vegetation is similar to areas much further north – open stands of stunted black spruce with an understory of dwarf birch, Labrador tea, lichen and moss. Many large treeless areas exist.

Around Lake Melville, a huge inland water body, magnificent stands of black spruce and balsam fir with an understory of feathermoss are common. This "high boreal" forest is valuable for wood pulp. The slow growth of the trees results in a denser fibre content and thus more wood pulp per unit volume than can be obtained from larger trees grown in more moderate climates.

tree cover is sparse and the area stands out as a large island of arctic tundra. The largest herd of barren-ground caribou in the region frequents the proposed park area.

Mealy Mountains

WILDLIFE:

Wildlife characteristic of the boreal forest thrives here: moose, caribou, black bear, red fox, lynx, snowshoe hare, wolf, spruce grouse, raven. Along the coast seabirds and waterfowl congregate, including Atlantic puffins, murres, petrels, gannets, Canada geese, eider ducks, and black ducks. Seals, whales and the occasional polar bear frequent the coast.

STATUS OF NATIONAL PARKS:

No national parks have yet been established in this region, although an area in the **Mealy Mountains** was proposed in 1977 as a possible national park. The Mealy Mountains rise steeply out of tidal Lake Melville, reaching heights of over 1200 metres. The highest peaks are snowcapped throughout most of the summer. In the mountains

In 1977 the Canadian Parks Service and the Government of Newfoundland and Labrador began discussions with the interested public concerning the feasibility of establishing a national park in this region, but it was decided to defer further consideration until negotiations began on the Naskapi-Montagnais-Innu Association comprehensive claim. The Labrador Inuit Association and Conseil Attikamek-Montagnais comprehensive claims also overlap the Mealy Mountains area.

Two other representative natural areas have been tentatively identified in this region: Red Bay and Natashquan/Romaine Rivers in Quebec.

Establishment of a national park in this natural region will require an agreement with the Government of Newfoundland and Labrador (or Quebec) and the support and co-operation of the Native people.

The following table summarizes the status of system planning for each step toward establishing a new national park in this natural region.

Steps in the Park Establishment Process	Status
Representative Natural Areas Identified:	done
Potential Park Area Selected:	done
Park Feasibility Assessed:	0
Park Agreement Signed:	0
Scheduled Under the National Parks Act:	0

22 Boreal Lake Plateau

Not represented

Labrador Tea

SPINDLY SPRUCE, ROCK AND ROARING RIVERS

The earth was created the way it was by the creator, and changing it is unnatural and wrong. The land and the rivers where the Cree people hunt and fish are a garden, a gift from the Creator...it has to be treated with love and respect to ensure that its spirit lives forever.

John Petagumskum,
Cree Elder, 1990.

Bog Rosemary

THE LAND:

An endless patchwork of interconnected lakes, rivers full of rapids and falls, bogs, swamps, spruce forests and treeless barrens — this is an elemental land, split between water and bedrock, softened by a thin veneer of spruce forest and muskeg. Many large rivers drain westward into Hudson and James bays, dropping in a series of steps over terraces marking ancient sea levels. Large lakes cover much of the region. The topography is gentle and undulating, broken occasionally by hills.

Natural Region 22

Guillaume-Delisle's Cuesta

VEGETATION:

The term "boreal" in the name of this region implies that the boreal forest ecosystem is a dominant feature. But actually the vegetation of the region is a south to north transition from dense spruce forests to muskeg. Fire occurs frequently and is a major influence on vegetation in this region.

Black spruce is the dominant tree species. Closed crown forests are restricted to lowlands around lakes and along rivers. Most of the land is covered by a drunken chequerboard pattern of open black spruce woodland, low shrubs, open muskeg and string bogs. As one moves towards the north of the region, the spruce become progressively more stunted and the stands more open. Shrubs such as dwarf birch, willow and Labrador tea cover a greater percentage of the land. Extensive poorly drained areas cover much of the region, with open wet black spruce woodlands, muskeg and string bogs stretching endlessly. From the air, string bogs appear as a series of sinuous light strips, like cooked spaghetti, floating across dark areas of open water.

The "strings" are actually ridges of sphagnum moss growing on accumulations of peat. String bogs form on very gradual slopes, with the "strings" stretched across the bog at right angles to the slope.

WILDLIFE:

Characteristic wildlife include caribou, moose, black bear, red fox, arctic fox, snowshoe hare, spruce grouse, wolf, coyote, beaver, mink, lynx, and marten, among other typical wildlife of northern regions. Waterfowl, particularly whistling swans, snow geese and Canada geese, congregate along the shores of James Bay and Hudson Bay each fall to feed. Belugas, bearded seals and harbour seals feed in the fertile waters offshore. Seals inhabit two inland lakes in the region, Lac-des-Loups-Marins and Petit-Lac-des-Loups-Marins, both of which are proposed ecological reserves. Whether these fresh-water seals are a separate species is under study.

String Bog

STATUS OF NATIONAL PARKS:

No national parks exist yet in this region. The **Lake Guillaume-Delisle** area has been identified as a potential representative natural area. Lake Guillaume-Delisle itself, once known as Richmond Gulf, is a vast brackish estuary linked to Hudson Bay by a narrow corridor. Outstanding features of this area include spectacular shoreline cliffs and the twin craters filled by Lac a l'Eau Claire (Clearwater

Field Party, Lake Gullaume-Delisle

Lake), the second largest natural lake in Quebec. The two adjoining craters are believed to be the remains of an ancient volcano or the result of a meteorite that split before hitting the earth. The Eau Claire River connecting the lake of the same name to Lake Guillaume-Delisle is a chain of cascades and falls of remarkable beauty. The tree line passes through the proposed park area.

In 1989 the mayor of Umiujaq, a community on Hudson Bay, asked the Canadian Parks Service to consider the possibility of establishing a national park in the Lake Guillaume-Delisle area. Lake Guillaume-Delisle lies within the area covered by the James Bay and Northern Quebec Agreements (1975-1980). These agreements, a result of the James Bay hydro-electric power projects, settled the question of aboriginal rights in the James Bay and Northern Quebec Territory. Besides monetary compensations, they provide for the participation of native peoples – the Cree, Inuit and Naskapis – in the management and development of the territory. A park proposal has yet to be developed.

Hydro-Québec is making final plans to develop La Grande Riviere de la Baleine, a major watershed

just to the south of the Lake Guillaume-Delisle area, for hydro-electric power. How this project, slated for completion in 1998, will affect the Lake Guillaume-Delisle watershed is not yet known.

The establishment of a new national park in the Lake Guillaume-Delisle area will require an agreement with the Government of Quebec and the people of Umiujaq.

The following table summarizes the status of system planning for each step toward establishing a new national park in this natural region.

Steps in the Park Establishment Process	Status
Representative Natural Areas Identified:	done
Potential Park Area Selected:	done
Park Feasibility Assessed:	0
Park Agreement Signed:	0
Scheduled Under the National Parks Act:	0

Lake Guillaume-Delisle

22

Caniapiscau River

THE OTHER BAY OF GIANT TIDES

The deer [caribou] are the property of a spirit. The spirit sends them every year to the barren ground to feed in the summer and in the fall he drives them back east, to put them in a mountain which is so high that no Indian can go to the top of it, where they remain all winter, sheltered from the weather. The mountain is guarded by ants as large as frogs, by frogs as large as foxes, by foxes as large as wolves.... Should this spirit find the pelt of a deer ... left to rot, he would be so angry that he would search the whole country and not leave one deer for the Indian who left the skin in such a manner....

As told to James Clouston,
explorer and furtrader,
by his guide in 1820.

Koksoak River

THE LAND:

A saucer-shaped depression, in places a featureless plain, this region is bordered on the west by the rugged Labrador Hills and on the east by the ancient granite hills of the George Plateau. The unyielding bedrock of the Canadian Shield underlies this area, though it is often hidden under glacial deposits and features such as drumlins and moraines. Permafrost is present throughout much of the region. Broad boulder mudflats fringe the coast of Ungava Bay, which boasts some of the world's highest tides (as great as 18 metres) and strongest tidal currents.

George River

sphagnum, northern Labrador tea and cotton grass are typical species growing on poorly drained areas.

WILDLIFE:

Several major caribou herds, whose numbers have increased in recent years

Caribou

VEGETATION:

The vegetation of this region is transitional between tundra and taiga. Most of the region south of Ungava Bay is covered by open stands of black spruce interspersed with dwarf birch, northern Labrador tea and lichens, with shrubs accounting for about 50 percent of the ground cover. Denser forests grow along the major river valleys. These trees are surprisingly large for being so close to the tree line. A larch over 23 metres high on the Koksoak River and many black spruce over 17 metres have been recorded.

Along the coast of Ungava Bay is a nearly continuous cover of dwarf tundra vegetation less than 30 centimetres tall. Paralleling this zone is a narrow band of vegetation characterized by very open stands of stunted black spruce and tamarack. Tundra vegetation covers the ground between the trees. Many of the trees are so stunted that they appear more like recumbent shrubs. A few vertical branches a metre or more in height, bare except for a few living sprigs at the tip, remind one that these are trees. Vast areas of bogs and fens occur throughout the region. Sedges,

to over 600 000 animals, make their home in this region, bearing their young on calving grounds in the south and migrating in late spring to their summer ranges in the north.

Other characteristic wildlife species include moose, black bear, beaver, snowshoe hare and arctic fox. Arctic char are abundant in all large rivers in the region, along with Atlantic salmon. The mud flats on Ungava Bay provide important nesting and moulting habitat for snow geese, Canada geese and other waterfowl.

STATUS OF NATIONAL PARKS:

No national parks have yet been established in this region. Completing a regional analysis to identify representative natural areas is the first step. Initial studies have suggested three areas that merit further consideration: **George River, Caniapiscau River** and **Koksoak River.** More detailed studies to confirm which of these best represents the region will be the next step toward establishing a national park.

Somewhere in Natural Region 23

All three areas are within the area covered by the James Bay and Northern Quebec Agreements (1975-1980). These agreements, a result of the James Bay hydro-electric power projects, settled the question of aboriginal rights in the James Bay and Northern Quebec Territory. Besides monetary compensations, they provide for the participation of native peoples – the Cree, Inuit and Naskapis – in the management and development of the territory.

Other factors that could influence park establishment include the hydro-electric power potential of these rivers and the high mineral potential of the Canadian Shield that underlies this region. Iron ore and nickel deposits have been discovered in the

Labrador Hills in the western part of the region, but these have not yet been developed.

The establishment of a new national park in this natural region will require an agreement with the Government of Quebec and the support and co-operation of local people.

The following table summarizes the status of system planning for each step toward establishing a new national park in this natural region.

Steps in the Park Establishment Process	Status
Representative Natural Areas Identified:	0
Potential Park Area Selected:	0
Park Feasibility Assessed:	0
Park Agreement Signed:	0
Scheduled Under the National Parks Act:	0

24 Northern Labrador Mountains

Not represented

Miriam Lake, Torngat Mountains

THE UNKNOWN EASTERN MOUNTAINS

Breath-taking fiords, jagged peaks rising abruptly from a frigid sea, icebergs, polar bears, glaciers .... some of the most spectacular coastscapes in the world are found in this natural region – unknown to all but the Innu.

THE LAND:

This region contains two distinct, contrasting landscapes: the George Plateau and the spectacular Torngat Mountains.

The George Plateau is a level bedrock plain cut by deep river valleys sloping gently to Ungava Bay. The effects of glaciation are ubiquitous: drumlin fields, kame terraces (ridges of water-born sediments deposited by melting glaciers), erratics and eskers that snake over the plateau like trails left by the huge sand worms on the fictional planet "Dune".

The Torngat Mountains, among the highest, most rugged mountains in eastern North America and one of the world's most beautiful wild coastlines, provide a spectacular counterpoint to the gentle George Plateau.

VEGETATION:

Forest-tundra, characterized by open stands of black spruce and tamarack with an understory of low-lying arctic shrubs, dominates the southern part of the region. As one moves north and climbs

Nachvak Fiord, Torngat Mountains

higher, the vegetation becomes sparse, consisting mainly of lichens, mosses, sedges, grasses and hardy arctic flowers. Shrubs such as willow and alder are limited to sheltered areas. Rock deserts with little vegetation other than lichens and a few low-lying hardy forbs cover large areas.

WILDLIFE:

Typical mammals include caribou, moose, black bear, red fox, arctic fox, snowshoe hare, wolf, coyote, beaver and muskrat. The George River caribou herd, estimated at 100 000 – 200 000 animals, ranges through much of the region. Polar bears patrol the coast, although they are much less common than in the past. Seabirds such as puffins, murres, razorbills and others frequent the rocky islands offshore. Whales – killer, fin, humpback, minke and blue – harbour and ringed seals and the occasional walrus frequent the coast.

STATUS OF NATIONAL PARKS:

No national parks exist yet in this region. In 1977, the Canadian Parks Service proposed the **Torngat Mountains** area as a new national park. This is one of the most dramatic landscapes in eastern North America. Fiords slash inland 30-80 kilometres. Cliffs up to 900 metres high rise abruptly from the sea. Icebergs, set adrift two years earlier in Greenland, float by. Inland, the Torngat Mountains, lonely and austere, rip the sky, their sharp peaks reaching elevations of over 1500 metres. These mountains resemble the western ranges in their ruggedness and scale. Broad U-shaped glacier-carved valleys, cirque lakes, glaciers, precipitous waterfalls – all these features are found in this mountainous region.

The Canadian Parks Service began discussions with the interested public concerning the feasibility of park establishment in 1977. During these discussions it became apparent that clarification of native land-claim issues was required before the park establishment process could continue. In 1979, further action relating to park feasibility assessment was suspended, pending negotiations of the

Labrador Inuit Association (LIA) comprehensive claim, which includes the proposed park area. The national park proposal will be among the items to be discussed in upcoming LIA claim negotiations.

Nachvak Lake

The establishment of a new national park in this natural region will require the concurrence of the Government of Newfoundland and Labrador and the Labrador Inuit Association.

The following table summarizes the status of system planning for each step toward establishing a new national park in this natural region.

Steps in the Park Establishment Process	Status
Representative Natural Areas Identified:	done
Potential Park Area Selected:	done
Park Feasibility Assessed:	0
Park Agreement Signed:	0
Scheduled Under the National Parks Act:	0

Not represented

Nastapoka Falls

SILENT, ENDLESS LAND

Scattered, patternless lakes, a litter of angular boulders and a pastel green and grey sweep of rock and low shrubs that goes on seemingly forever without change – silent except for the screams of circling hawks.

THE LAND:

This is a vast wild plateau, strewn with low granite hills and strewn with boulders. The region is underlain by the bedrock of the Canadian Shield, which lies exposed over much of the land; in other places it is smoothed by a thin veneer of glacial drift. At the coast of Hudson Strait, the plateau stops abruptly, plunging precipitously as much as 600 metres to the sea.

The New Quebec Crater, the most spectacular and well-defined meteorite impact crater in Canada, is found in this region. This is a "simple crater" – a circular depression 400 metres deep in solid granite and 3 kilometres across, surrounded by walls over 150 metres high. One of the clearest lakes in the world fills much of the crater.

The climate is rigorous. There are really only two seasons – a long, bitterly cold winter and a brief cool summer. The lowest monthly temperature is never above freezing point. Snow lies from the end of September to the end of June, and in deeper ravines as late as the middle of July.

VEGETATION:

This region is characterized by a nearly continuous cover of dwarf tundra vegetation, usually less than 30 centimetres tall. Creeping

Hudson Bay Coast

black spruce, dwarf birch, willow and woody shrubs such as northern Labrador tea, blueberry, crowberry, bearberry and dryas are conspicuous species. In the brief fall, the leaves of the low arctic shrubs carpet the tundra in brilliant shades of red and orange.

WILDLIFE:

Caribou find important summer range and calving grounds in this region. Other conspicuous land mammals include the wolf, arctic fox, red fox and lemming. Waterfowl such as Canada geese and snow geese nest and moult throughout the region. Willow and rock ptarmigan are plentiful.

Ptarmigan, along with ravens, are the only birds remaining here all year round. Hawks, particularly the rough-legged hawk and gyrfalcon, wheel and soar through the air on the lookout for lemmings or young ptarmigan. Snow buntings and Lapland longspurs flit silently among the lichen-covered boulders, stuffing their beaks with mosquitoes and gnats. Thick-billed murre and other seabirds nest on the cliffs along the north coast of the region. There are about 800 000 thick-billed murres at Digges Island and Cape Wolstenholme, the biggest colonies of this species in Canada.

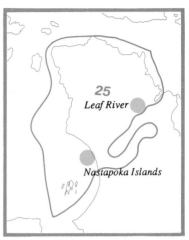

Leaf River

STATUS OF NATIONAL PARKS:

No national parks have yet been established in this region. Two possible areas have been identified – **Leaf River** and **Nastapoka** – but field studies are needed to confirm the degree to which these sites represent the natural region.

The Leaf River Estuary on Ungava Bay is the site of the highest tides in the world (18 metres). Broad tidal flats provide feeding and nesting areas for Canada geese and other waterfowl. Caribou and a small herd of muskoxen inhabit the inland areas. The Nastapoka area on the shore of Hudson Bay includes a chain of offshore islands, gentle grassy shorelines and timeless barrens. The Nastapoka River is within the area affected by Hydro-Québec's La Grande Rivière de la Baleine hydro-electric project.

The two areas (except for the Nastapoka Islands which are under the jurisdiction of the Northwest Territories) are covered by the James Bay and Northern Quebec Agreements (1975-1980). These agreements, a result of the James Bay hydro-electric power projects, settled the question of aboriginal rights in the James Bay and Northern Quebec Territory. Besides monetary compensations, they provide for the participation of native peoples – the Cree, Inuit and Naskapis – in the management and development of the territory.

The establishment of a new national park in this natural region will require an agreement with the Government of Quebec and the support and co-operation of native people.

The following table summarizes the status of system planning for each step toward establishing a new national park in this natural region.

Steps in the Park Establishment Process	Status
Representative Natural Areas Identified:	done
Potential Park Area Selected:	0
Park Feasibility Assessed:	0
Park Agreement Signed:	0
Scheduled Under the National Parks Act :	0

26 Northern Davis Region

Represented by: Auyuittuq National Park Reserve

"THE LAND THAT NEVER MELTS"

The Ice Age still grips this region of jagged peaks, deep fiords, looming glaciers and massive ice caps. But there is also a delicate beauty here ... pastel tundra flowers, soft mossy meadows, sparkling streams of glacial meltwater.

Bylot Island

THE LAND:

Ice and rock reign supreme in this natural region. The northern portion of the region is blanketed by thick ice caps and glaciers, smoothing the unevenness of the bedrock below. Tongues of ice touch the sea, calving glaciers into dark waters.

The east coast of Baffin Island presents a different

Mt. Thor, Auyuittuq National Park Reserve

face. This is a land of spectacular mountains, glaciers, deep fiords and the massive Penny Ice Cap. Here can be found classic alpine glacial scenery, the best in Canada and, in the opinion of some climbers, the best in the world.

A third face of this natural region is seen on western Baffin Island, where the mountains slope down to meet the coast in a low lake-studded coastal plain. In contrast to the east side, the coast is low, and broad intertidal flats are typical.

The southern part of Baffin Island presents a fourth face – a high rocky plateau.

VEGETATION:

Vegetation ranges from very patchy and open to lush tundra meadows. The broken rock of glacial moraines supports a scanty cover of lichens, with mosses and cushion plants such as moss campion, purple saxifrage and mountain avens nestling in the low spots. Cushion plants can thrive in the harsh arctic environment by creating their own micro-climate. The temperature within the dense mass of leaves is several degrees higher than the ambient temperature. The fragile-looking arctic poppy sends its cheery yellow flower up to 30 centimetres above even the most barren areas.

Mt. Asgard

In the southern areas of Baffin Island, lush tundra vegetation is found. Arctic shrubs such as dwarf birch, willow, heather, and blueberry and their berry-bearing kin form a continuous colourful carpet in sheltered valleys. On less favourable areas, tundra covered by tussocks of grasses and sedges makes for one of the most difficult walking surfaces known.

WILDLIFE:

Although most of this region is ice and rock, several highly productive land areas, bordered by rich marine environments, exist. The lush tundra supports land mammals such as arctic hare, lemming, wolf, arctic fox, red fox and caribou. Polar bear, walrus, beluga, narwhal and several species of seal (ringed, bearded, hooded) are common in the offshore waters. The waters of Lancaster Sound, off the north tip of Baffin Island, are unusually productive, harbouring large populations of many species of marine mammals and seabirds.

The cliffs of Bylot Island north of Baffin Island and the Hall Peninsula at its southern tip support huge rookeries of northern fulmars, thick-billed murres, black-legged kittiwakes and other seabirds. The largest northern fulmar colony known, containing between 200 000 and 500 000 birds, is found on Cape Searle on the east coast of Baffin Island. Two Migratory Bird Sanctuaries, Bylot Island and Cape Dorset, protect seabird colonies.

STATUS OF NATIONAL PARKS:

Auyuittuq – "the land that never melts" – **National Park Reserve** (21 471 km²)is a rugged wilderness park. Actually, each summer the land does melt – but only at its edges. Water pours from the snouts of glaciers, and a few inches of soil above the permafrost turns into a slurry of mud and gravel. The massive Penny Ice Cap takes up much of the park interior, spawning glaciers that are still actively shaping the land. The glacier-carved peaks and the Akshayuk Pass hiking route attract adventurers from around the world. Auyuittuq includes a 1141-square-kilometre marine component encompassing the fiords along the northern portion of the park. The area was proclaimed as a park reserve in 1976 subject to settlement of the Tungavik Federation of Nunavut comprehensive claim.

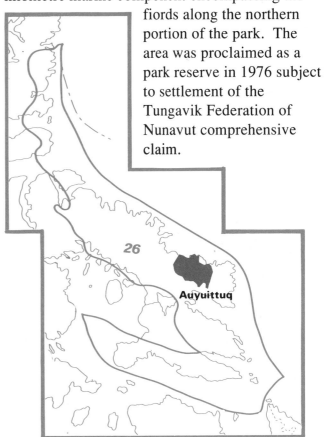

27 Hudson-James Lowlands

Prince of Wales' Fort

ENDLESS HORIZONS

...Though only at the distance of two miles, so low and flat was the land, that it appeared ten miles off, and scarcely a tree was to be seen....

The words of R.M. Ballantyne, a clerk with the Hudson's Bay Company, upon sighting this region.

Wet Tundra, Churchill Area

THE LAND:

The entire region is a vast sodden plain that slopes gently toward the sea at a gradient of less than a metre per kilometre. Up to 85 percent of the region is muskeg or peat-forming wetlands. Such a huge expanse of peat occurs nowhere else in North America and in only a few places in the world.

This is a land more of water than earth. Water lies everywhere – shallow oblong lakes, rivers that meander endlessly, streams running nowhere, bogs and fens; up to 50 percent of the surface is covered by water. Water in the form of permafrost underlies much of the region, resulting in landforms such as patterned ground, string bogs and palsas (mounds of frozen peat). In summer, walking is torture. At every step the muskeg sucks at your feet while hordes of insects suck your blood. Possibly nowhere else on earth are biting and sucking insects more abundant.

Since the retreat of the ice sheets, the land has been rebounding – like a piece of foam that expands when a weight is removed. Rising almost a metre a century, one of the fastest rates in the world, much of the region is newly emerged, less than 4,000 years old.

VEGETATION:

Approaching from sea as the first Europeans did, one sees a treeless land. Outside of alpine areas this is one of the most southerly expanses of tundra in the world. Separating the treeless tundra from the boreal forest is a mosaic of forest and tundra. Farther inland, dense forests of white spruce, balsam fir, aspen, balsam poplar and white birch occur on well-drained riverbanks and lake shores. Black spruce and tamarack spread over vast expanses of poorly drained muskeg.

Willow Ptarmigan

WILDLIFE:

The region is famous for its polar bears. A unique characteristic of this most southerly population of polar bears is that they construct summer dens to cool off in. Some are more than six metres deep and have probably been used for centuries. Caribou concentrate along the coastline in summer and winter inland among the boreal forests. In summer the coast of this region is alive with birds. Lesser snow geese, small Canada geese, brant, whistling swans, oldsquaw, king eider, northern phalarope and a host of shorebirds nest here.

STATUS OF NATIONAL PARKS:

Two representative natural areas, **Cape Churchill/ York Factory** and **Attawapiskat River/Akimiski Island** have been identified in this region. In 1989, the Canadian Parks Service, province of Manitoba and town of Churchill began assessing the feasibility of establishing a national park in the Cape Churchill/York Factory area. The study area includes the largest known polar bear denning habitat in the world and is one of the most accessible places known to view polar bears. The Hudson Bay coastline provides critical waterfowl and shorebird nesting and feeding habitat. Thousands of beluga rear their young and feed in the clear, shallow waters of river estuaries offshore from the park study area. Four sites of national historic significance are found here, including York Factory, for nearly three centuries the Hudson's Bay Company's principal fur trade centre, and the ruins of Fort Prince of Wales, a huge stone fortification built by the Hudson's Bay Company in the 1700s. Two Provincial Wildlife Management Areas, Cape Churchill and Cape Tatnam, are included within the national park study area.

Factors affecting the feasibility of a park include the resolution of land use issues such as hunting, trapping, recreation, settlement of specific land claims under Treaty 5, and assessment of tourism

Attawapiskat River

James Bay Lowlands

and related economic benefits associated with a national park. If a national park is shown to be feasible and to have sufficient support, the next step will be to reach a federal-provincial agreement for the establishment of a national park.

Establishment of a national park will require the support and co-operation of the residents of the Churchill region and the Government of Manitoba.

The following table summarizes the status of system planning for each step toward establishing a new national park in this natural region.

Steps in the Park Establishment Process	Status
Representative Natural Areas Identified:	done
Potential Park Area Selected:	done
Park Feasibility Assessed:	in progress
Park Agreement Signed:	0
Scheduled Under the National Parks Act:	0

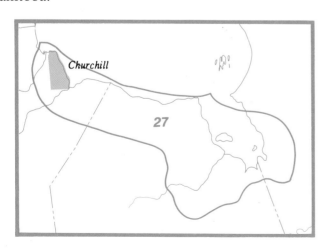

28 Southampton Plain

Not represented

Southampton Island

BY THE BAY OF GOD'S MERCY

The world is transformed, within a week or two, from a silent expanse to a place of amazing activity and noise. Everywhere the sounds of mating birds mingle with the cracking of ice along the shore, the roar of swelling streams and the laughter of Eskimo children... Lemmings ... bask in the sun ... butterflies wander about, the green grass shoots up, the willow catkins expand and droop....

George Sutton,
naturalist and explorer, 1924,
describing June on Southampton Island.

THE LAND:

This relatively small natural region includes part of Southampton Island, two other large islands and several smaller islands in the northern part of Hudson Bay. The combination of limestone and dolomite bedrock and dwarf arctic shrub vegetation makes this region distinct.

The coastal plain is low lying with many small lakes, marshes, wet meadows and broad tidal flats. Raised beaches, evidence of higher sea levels in the past and the rebounding of the land after being released from the weight of the glaciers, parallel the coast. Much of this region was flooded after the retreat of the glaciers, effectively obliterating glacial landforms except for a few scattered eskers. Inland are large limestone plateaux covered by frost-shattered rock where little life is found.

Coats Island

VEGETATION:

The barrens here are truly barren; large areas support only scattered clumps of the shrub dryas, its white blossoms brightening the shattered limestone that covers the ground. Much of the coast is devoid of vegetation. However, comparatively lush wet meadows of sedges and willows and rich tidal marshes occur where rivers enter the sea. Large grassy meadows also occur in the interior. In sheltered areas along river valleys, willows, the only "tree" occurring in this region, may reach two metres in height.

WILDLIFE:

Most of the mammals living here – arctic hare, lemmings, short-tailed weasel, arctic fox, polar bear and caribou – are species characteristic of the Arctic. Caribou and wolves were killed off on Southampton Island in the 1950s. However, caribou have been reintroduced and appear to be thriving.

The large walrus population found in this region is a distinguishing feature. Although they spend much of their time on the ice pack, the walruses find important hauling out grounds throughout the region.

Walrus

Shorebirds and waterfowl are abundant along the wet coastal meadows and tidal flats. Some of Canada's largest colonies of snow geese and Canada geese, along with the rare Ross's goose, nest in the rich sedge meadows of the Boas River Delta. The Harry Gibbons Migratory Bird Sanctuary (1489 km2) on Southampton Island protects the nesting site of over 300 000 snow geese. Large colonies of thick-billed murres are found on Coates Island, one of the large offshore islands in Hudson Bay.

STATUS OF NATIONAL PARKS:

No national parks exist yet in this region. Studies to identify representative natural areas need to be undertaken. The planning of a national park must

take into consideration the fact that hunting, trapping and fishing, the traditional land uses of the Arctic, are still carried on in this region. Seals, walrus, beluga, polar bear and caribou are the main species hunted; trapping for arctic fox provides income for many residents.

Establishment of a national park in this natural region will require the support and co-operation of the residents of Coral Harbour, the Tungavik Federation of Nunavut and the Government of the Northwest Territories.

The following table summarizes the status of system planning for each step toward establishing a new national park in this natural region.

Steps in the Park Establishment Process	Status
Representative Natural Areas Identified:	0
Potential Park Area Selected:	0
Park Feasibility Assessed:	0
Park Agreement Signed:	0
Scheduled Under the National Parks Act:	0

Represented by: Bruce Peninsula National Park; Mingan Archipelago National Park Reserve; Georgian Bay Islands National Park (part); Point Pelee National Park

Monarch Butterfly, Point Pelee National Park

CANADA'S DEEP SOUTH

At Arnall's Creek they found a flat marsh-grass quite free from forest trees which were then universal above the water's edge of Lake Ontario. Here they pitched their tents, the creek and lake forming two sides of a triangle for defence from wolves... Salmon would run in November, and the winter supply of fish secured from the creek....

From an account of the first settlers near where Toronto now stands.

THE LAND:

This natural region comprises three widely separated units linked by the unfolded sedimentary bedrock that underlies them. Although each unit shares a common geological origin, the geographical distances between them and the disparity in intensity of land use and population density produces a lack of uniformity with respect to flora and fauna and the impact of human activities on the land. The western and central units are among the most human-altered regions of Canada, containing about half the population of Canada; the eastern unit is largely unsettled.

The Niagara Escarpment, a line of cliffs and bluffs up to 300 metres high snaking across the entire western unit from Georgian Bay to the Niagara River, is the most prominent landform in a region of gentle unspectacular relief. The Niagara River cuts through the escarpment at Niagara Falls and Gorge, one of the most outstanding examples of a falls and gorge in Canada, and certainly the most photographed.

Flowerpot Island, Georgian Bay Islands National Park

The story of the most recent glaciation is written heavily on the region. Large drumlin fields, boulder-studded moraines and thick deposits of glacial till (such as the Scarborough Bluffs near Toronto) dominate the topography of the region.

VEGETATION AND WILDLIFE:

Of all the natural regions in Canada, this region encompasses the greatest biodiversity. Five biogeographic zones are found in this region: Carolinian forest, deciduous forest and mixedwood forest in the western and central units; mid-boreal and high-boreal forests in the eastern unit.

Wood Duck

The Carolinean zone, restricted in Canada to the western unit of Region 29, is characterized by flora and fauna whose ranges extend far to the south. The most diverse flora and fauna in Canada are found here.

Cape May Warbler

Although the vegetation is typified by a broadleaf forest of sugar maple, American beech, basswood, white oak, red oak, shagbark hickory, black walnut and butternut, farm fields and man-altered sites are the norm today. Wildlife that thrives in this zone today must be able to take advantage of agricultural crops and suburban habitats. Many common species, such as white-tailed deer, grey squirrel, coyote, starling, house sparrow and ringbilled gull, are recent arrivals to this region. Reptiles include several endangered species (eastern spiny soft-shelled turtle,

Blanding's turtle, box turtle, and fox snake, among others) and eastern Canada's only lizard, the five-lined skink.

The climax forest in the deciduous forest zone is dominated by sugar maple and American beech, with hemlock dominant on shady north-facing slopes. White pine, red pine and red oak dominate the dry ridge tops. In the mixedwood forest zone, undisturbed sites consist of sugar maple, yellow birch, eastern hemlock and white pine. Boreal species such as white spruce, black spruce and balsam fir dominate in cool, damp habitats. Moose, wolf, snowshoe hare, martin, spruce grouse and other boreal species intermix with species more typical of southern areas such as the cardinal, white-tailed deer and raccoon.

The eastern unit is characterized by boreal forests of black spruce, jack pine, balsam fir and white birch. Wildlife is boreal: wolf, caribou, lynx, martin, spruce grouse, snowshoe hare. Thousands of snow geese congregate on the tidal flats of Cap Tourmente National Wildlife Area on the shore of the St. Lawrence Estuary during migration.

Ile Niapiskau, Mingan Archipelago National Park Reserve

STATUS OF NATIONAL PARKS:

Three national parks and one national park reserve represent this region. **Point Pelee National Park** (16 km²), a Ramsar site (wetland of international significance), is renowned as Canada's finest bird-watching site. A sandspit at the southernmost tip of Canada's mainland, Point Pelee is a unique blend of marsh, forest, fields and beach, which combined with its southern extension into Lake Erie, attracts thousands of birds and monarch butterflies on their biannual migrations. The forests of Point Pelee are jungle-like in appearance and harbour an unusually large variety of trees typical of the Carolinean zone. Point Pelee was established in 1918 from Naval Reserve lands after resolutions were submitted to the federal government recommending the preservation of Point Pelee as a wildlife sanctuary.

Bruce Peninsula National Park (270 km²) is the subject of a 1987 federal-provincial agreement with the Government of Ontario that involved the transfer of two existing provincial parks, Cypress Lake and Fathom Five, and the acquisition of private lands on a "willing buyer-willing seller" basis. The area is a spectacular yet fragile land of rare orchids, limestone cliffs and weirdly eroded rock formations. The Bruce Trail, a popular hiking trail hugging the edge of the Niagara Escarpment, is adjacent to Canada's first National Marine Park, Fathom Five, where transparent waters and more than 20 wrecks beckon intrepid divers. These parks will be proclaimed under the

National Parks Act once the lands are formally transferred to the Crown in right of Canada.

The part of **Georgian Bay Islands National Park** extending into this natural region includes several limestone islands off the Bruce Peninsula. The largest, Flowerpot Island, is named for unusual "flowerpot" rock formations, the result of receding water levels and constant wave action, which have eroded the soft limestone bedrock.

Oddly-shaped rock pillars sculpted by wind and sea create the unique island-scape of **Mingan Archipelago National Park Reserve** (151 km²). Puffins and other seabirds nest on these limestone islands in the Gulf of St. Lawrence, while porpoises, seals and whales feed in the fertile waters offshore. Mingan was set aside as a national park reserve in 1984, pending the resolution of the comprehensive land claim of the Attikamek-Montagnais.

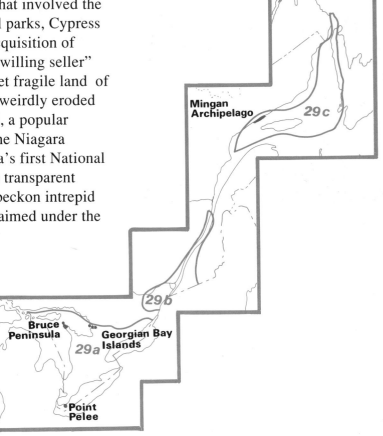

30 Notre Dame and Megantic Mountains

Represented by: Forillon National Park

STRIKING CONTRAST OF COAST AND MOUNTAINS

From the brilliant red-hued jutting cliffs of the Gaspé to the sombre, barren peaks of the Shickshock Mountains, this region, long renowned for its scenery, has been shaped by glaciers, by the unceasing gnawing of the sea and, most recently, by the hand of man.

Forillon National Park

Gannets, Bonaventure Island

THE LAND:

The ancient Appalachian Mountains form the backbone of this region. These worn, plateau-like flat-topped mountains, many with summits over 900 metres, compose the most spectacular, accessible mountain scenery in Canada east of the Rockies. The peaks are barren and covered with broken shale. Mount Jacques Cartier is the highest, at 1320 metres. Rivers have cut deep gorges through these ranges, widened during the most recent glaciation into magnificent U-shaped valleys. At the tip of the Gaspé Peninsula, the mountains meet the sea in a series of spectacular multi-hued cliffs and plunging headlands.

VEGETATION:

Highly variable, the vegetation of this region includes isolated populations of species normally expected far to the north and south. The highest peaks and exposed cliffs provide habitat for several arctic-alpine species normally found thousands of kilometres away in the Rockies or the Arctic – relics from a time when arctic conditions were prevalent throughout this region.

In the central chain of mountains, high elevations and strong maritime influences combine to produce a forest dominated by conifers. White spruce, balsam fir and black spruce, with an understory of feather moss, form a continuous cover except on the higher, more exposed peaks, where rock barrens and krummholtz (thickets of stunted twisted spruce and fir) occur. In the river valleys and at lower elevations, the vegetation has a southern flavour. Sugar maple, white pine and eastern hemlock form a rich mixedwood forest. Dry sites are characterized by red oak, red pine and white pine; wet sites by red maple, black ash and eastern white cedar.

WILDLIFE:

"In the Gaspé the hunter does not lack as often game as shot and powder."

This statement from a late nineteenth-century tourist brochure gives an indication of the past wealth of wildlife in this area. Like the vegetation, the wildlife shows marked influences from both north and south. Caribou, which once flourished throughout the central mountains, have been gone for over a century except for an isolated

Cap Bon Ami, Forillon National Park

herd in Gaspésie Provincial Park. The wolf and wolverine have also disappeared from the region. Species such as moose, black bear, red fox, lynx, snowshoe hare and others that thrive in boreal forests followed the retreat of the glaciers. Others, such as white-tailed deer, coyotes and groundhogs, moved into the region after settlers had cleared the land for farms and towns.

The red-walled cliffs and islets are home to thousands of sea and coastal birds. Bonaventure Island, one of many Migratory Bird Sanctuaries found in this region, supports a colony of gannets, common murres and a few puffins. Gulls, black guillemots, razorbills, double-crested cormorants and black-legged kittiwakes nest on narrow ledges and atop cliffs. Along the south shore of the St. Lawrence, flocks of migrating waterfowl congregate on the tidal flats.

STATUS OF NATIONAL PARKS

Forillon National Park (240 km^2) represents the Notre Dame Mountains and the boreal forest and coastal zone elements of this region. It includes a 160-metre-wide marine component extending along the coast. The park is noted for its abundance of marine mammals and birds. Double-crested cormorants, black guillemots, black-legged kittiwakes and razorbills nest on the coastal cliffs. Atlantic puffins, Leach's petrels and common murres feed in the fertile waters offshore. Harbour and grey seals regularly haul out on shoals and rocky points, while many species of whales – harbour porpoises, pilot whales, minke, sei, finback and humpback – are often seen from shore.

The richness of the sea has always been linked to man's presence here. The first European explorers found Micmac and Iroquois who had travelled here in summer to fish. In the eighteenth century, fishing villages based on the export of dried cod to Europe and the Caribbean were established along the coast. The traditional lifestyle of the cod fishermen of this region is a major focus of the park's interpretation program. Forillon was established in 1970 pursuant to a federal-provincial agreement with the Government of Quebec.

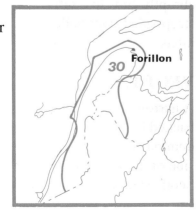

31 Maritime Acadian Highlands

Represented by: Fundy National Park; Cape Breton Highlands National Park

TIDES AND TRAILS

On the coast, a water world where fog often shrouds the shore and the mist hangs cold and damp from the sharp-pointed spruce; inland, a tranquil world of sun-dappled forests, hidden waterfalls, secluded glens and eternal barrens.

Pilot Whales, Cape Breton Highlands National Park

THE LAND:

A rolling plateau, a remnant of the ancient Caledonia Highlands, distinguishes this region. Averaging more than 300 metres above sea level, the plateau is cut by deep valleys and cascading rivers.

Scoured by the giant tides of the Bay of Fundy and pounded by Atlantic swells, this region meets the sea with drama and conflict. The Fundy shore alternates between tide-scoured cliffs of sedimentary rock and extensive mud flats and salt marshes. Around Cape Breton Island, the land abruptly ends in a series of bold headlands and steep-sided river valleys pouring into coves and inlets.

VEGETATION:

A narrow coastal strip 3-30 kilometres wide, backed by steeply rising uplands, supports a forest dominated by red spruce on the New Brunswick side of the Bay and by white spruce on the Nova Scotia shore. Inland, shady forests of white and

yellow birch, American beech and sugar maple, carpeted with a lush understory of ferns, provide a restful contrast to the dense, damp evergreen forests. Hemlock, red maple, white birch, red spruce and white pine are found at lower elevations. In the Cape Breton Island portion of the region, extensive "barrens," waist-high with Labrador tea and broken by pink granite outcroppings and patches of light green lichens, cover the upland plateau . Almost the entire region has been logged, some of it several times.

Alma Marsh, Fundy National Park

WILDLIFE:

Large mammals found in this region include white-tailed deer, moose, red fox, black bear, raccoon, bobcat, coyote, mink, otter, muskrat and beaver. Wolf and caribou once roamed this region, but disappeared early in the twentieth century.

Atlantic Puffins, Machias Seal Island

The salt marshes and tidal mud flats provide critical feeding and staging areas for myriads of shorebirds and waterfowl. Millions of semi-palmated sandpipers blacken beaches and mud flats in late summer to "re-fuel" for the long non-stop flight to South America. The Tantramarre marshes at the head of the Bay of Fundy are renowned for the vast numbers of waterfowl, particularly Canada geese, that gather here to feed in the rich salt marshes. The term "tantramarre" may be derived from an Acadian word referring to the racket made by the birds. Much of the extensive salt marshes have long been diked, drained and transformed into hay fields.

STATUS OF NATIONAL PARKS:

Two national parks represent this region, **Cape Breton Highlands** (951 km²) and **Fundy** (206 km²), established by federal-provincial agreements in 1936 and 1948 respectively. Fundy has two faces: the coast where tides alternately expose and submerge a damp ribbon of mudflats, salt marshes and tidal pools – an area not part of the land yet not entirely belonging to the sea; and the inland face, the Fundy of shady forests and tumbling streams. This park is characteristic of the rugged Bay of Fundy coast and the Caledonia

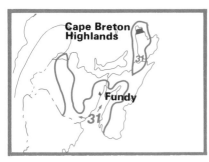

Highlands of southern New Brunswick. The park has a long history of human use; most of it has been logged in the past, and many old fields remain from small farms. The pine martin, considered rare in Canada, and a breeding population of peregrine falcons, an endangered species, have been reintroduced into the park.

The scenic Cabot Trail, the best-known feature of Cape Breton Highlands National Park, hugs the rim of the mountains, providing breathtaking views of the restless Gulf of St. Lawrence. Trails lead through a variety of habitats typical of this natural region – from lush hardwood forests carpeted with ferns, through boreal forests of spruce and fir and bogs dotted with orchids, to sub-arctic barrens and muskeg. The rock vole, Gaspé shrew, pygmy shrew and pine martin, all considered rare in Canada, occur in the park.

Weir

32 Maritime Plain

*Represented by: Prince Edward Island National Park,
Kouchibouguac National Park*

Barrier Island

Prince Edward Island National Park

THE LAND:

This is a gentle land. The surface slopes gently toward the sea, riding on horizontal strata of red sandstone, shale, conglomerates and mudstones. Where land meets sea are dune-edged beaches, salt marshes and warm lagoons. Offshore, a constantly shifting chain of barrier islands and reefs protects the shore from the fury of storms sweeping in from the Gulf of St. Lawrence.

SAND DUNES AND TEEMING ESTUARIES

Salt marshes rimmed by placid lagoons and endless ribbons of sun-swept sand beaches blend into dark forests and tidy farmlands. Canada's warmest ocean waters and longest beaches make this region a magnet for vacationers. "The finest land one can see, and full of beautiful trees and meadows...", wrote Jacques Cartier in 1534 upon landing on Prince Edward Island.

VEGETATION:

...the trees are wonderfully beautiful and fragrant ...we discovered there were cedars, yew-trees, pines, white elms, ash trees, willows and others...
Jacques Cartier, 1534

Very little of this region's original forest remains. The huge white pines described by Cartier and other explorers were largely gone by the end of the eighteenth century, cut down for masts for sailing ships. The original mixed wood forest of sugar maple, American beech, American elm, black ash, yellow birch, white pine and eastern hemlock has long been cleared for farms. Repeated logging, fires, insect epidemics and hurricanes have left only remnants of the original forest. Today, white spruce, black spruce, balsam fir and tamarack predominate. Large areas of muck and peat soils are present. Extensive salt marshes fringe the shore. The barrier islands and dunes are sparsely vegetated. Marram grass is the only plant that can initially

Kouchibouguac National Park

colonize the dunes, stabilizing the shifting sands and enabling other species to become established.

WILDLIFE:

The extensive beaches and sand-dune systems provide critical nesting habitat for the piping plover, an endangered species. Common terns nest on the barrier islands. The lagoons, beaches and salt marshes are frequented by many species of ducks and shorebirds. Great blue herons stalk the salt marshes and shorelines.

Common mammals include white-tailed deer, snowshoe hare, black bear, porcupine and red fox. Moose are scarce. Grey seals and harbour seals frequent the lagoons and estuaries. As most of the region has been logged or farmed, species dependent on mature forests, such as wolf, caribou, marten and fisher, have disappeared. Coyotes have recently arrived, a new predator in the region.

Many of this region's rivers have runs of Atlantic salmon. The most famous is the Mirimichi, one of the richest Atlantic salmon rivers in eastern North America. But pollution from pulp and paper mills and mines threatens to reduce the run.

STATUS OF NATIONAL PARKS:

Two national parks represent this natural region. At **Kouchibouguac National Park** (239 km²), established by a federal-provincial agreement in 1969 with the Government of New Brunswick, salt marshes rimmed by placid lagoons and sand dunes of the offshore barrier islands gently blend into evergreen forests concealing bogs and cedar swamps. Piping plovers, an endangered species, and common terns nest on the beaches and barrier islands. Striped bass spawn in the estuaries. Much of the park has been logged and farmed in the past, and accordingly much of the forest is in an early successional stage. Several rivers gently flowing across the park inspired its Micmac name – "River of the long tides".

Sand dunes, red sandstone cliffs and endless sand beaches characterise **Prince Edward Island National Park** (26 km²). Established in 1937 by federal legislation, the park is a dynamic system of shifting sand carried by wind and waves. Ponds and marshes develop inland of sand spits and provide habitat for the many birds that nest here, including the endangered piping plover. Perhaps the best-known feature of the park is Green Gables House, made famous internationally through Lucy Maud Montgomery's classic novel, "Anne of Green Gables".

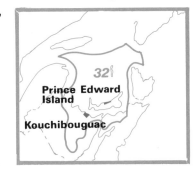

33 Atlantic Coast Uplands

Represented by: Kejimkujik National Park

GENTLE WATERS, LUSH FORESTS AND A POSTCARD COAST

A rugged yet gentle land of boulder-strewn barrens, tranquil forests, softly flowing rivers and shallow rock-studded lakes, framed by a rock-girded sea coast of world-renowned beauty.

Mersey River, Kejimkujik National Park

THE LAND:

From the coast, the land gradually rises to a height of about 200 metres in a series of irregular waves of folded metamorphic rock. The Ice Age has left its footprints on much of the region, scraping away the fertility of the land and depositing it in the sea where today it nurtures rich fisheries. Coarse, stony, shallow soils, exposed bedrock polished and grooved by the crawling glaciers, and erratics strewn about like glacier-scats are the legacy left by the Ice Age. Rivers and streams and thousands of shallow, rocky lakes are found throughout the region.

Kejimkujik's Seaside Adjunct

VEGETATION:

Along a band of coastline 3-30 kilometres wide are dense, stunted forests of balsam fir, black spruce and white spruce. The growth of trees along the coast is slow because of the marginal soil, harsh climate and salt spray. White spruce, which are salt-tolerant, dominate along the most exposed areas. Large areas of bare rock, bogs and barren lands have resulted from repeated fires. Isolated stands of old-growth hemlock forest are found throughout the region. Inland, mixed wood forests of red spruce, white pine, red oak and red maple are typical on well-drained sites. Although the combination of soil and climate is more conducive to growing trees here than it is along the coast, large barren areas and areas covered by low shrubs are still found. Fire and wind strongly influence the appearance of the vegetation in this region.

WILDLIFE:

Common large mammals include moose, white-tailed deer, black bear, snowshoe hare, red fox, porcupine, beaver, raccoon, marten and fisher. Before the turn of the century, caribou were plentiful throughout the region. But the combination of fires, agriculture, logging and settlement changed the region to a patchwork of forests, barrens and human habitations – ideal for moose and white-tailed deer but not for caribou.

Common Merganser

Salt marshes and tidal mud flats provide feeding and resting habitat for migrating waterfowl and shorebirds. The offshore frieze of islands and the indented coastline provide a rich habitat for gulls, cormorants, terns, guillemots and other coastal birds. The numerous lakes and streams are famous for speckled trout and runs of Atlantic salmon. "The angler may obtain such sport as he perhaps never dreamed of", an eighteenth century guide to Nova Scotia said of fishing in this region.

Kejimkujik National Park

STATUS OF NATIONAL PARKS:

The inland portion of this region is represented by **Kejimkujik National Park** (384 km^2), established pursuant to a federal-provincial agreement with the Government of Nova Scotia in 1967. The island-studded lakes and smooth-flowing rivers of this park are linked by a network of canoe trails used for thousands of years by the Micmac Indians. Hiking trails wind through rounded hills and shady forests where groves of 300-year-old hemlock trees can still be found. Several outstanding petroglyph sites depict elements of Micmac and European culture.

The coastal elements of this natural region are represented by the Kejimkujik's coastal adjunct, the **Port Mouton** lands (22 km^2). Pursuant to a federal-provincial agreement with the

Government of Nova Scotia, this area was added to the park in 1988 as one of the amendments to the National Parks Act introduced through Bill C-30. One of the least-disturbed shoreline areas on the south coast of Nova Scotia, the Port Mouton lands feature extensive brackish ponds and broad tidal flats. The endangered piping plover nests on the beaches of this peninsula. Dense scrub, century-old spruce-fir forests and barren uplands provide a backdrop to the shoreline.

34 Western Newfoundland Highlands

Represented by: Gros Morne National Park

Western Brook Pond, Gros Morne National Park

IN THE LAND OF TUCKAMOOR

The numberless waterfalls and cascades will cause surprise to those who ... believe Newfoundland to be a flat land of bogs and rocks.... People have not the slightest idea of what wonderful scenery is hidden away ... only waiting to be discovered.

A.A. Radclyffe Dugmore, 1913
British Author and Sportsman

Bonne Bay, Gros Morne National Park

THE LAND:

Driving up the coast from the ferry terminal at Port Aux Basques, at the southern extremity of this natural region, the highway is squeezed between the clear green waters and white sand beaches of the Gulf of St. Lawrence and the looming, blue-shadowed Long Range Mountains. Spectacular fiords slash inland. The Long Range Mountains form the backbone of this region, sloping gently toward the Atlantic to the east, and dropping precipitously toward the west into the Gulf.

VEGETATION:

In the southern portion of the region, forests of balsam fir, with some black spruce and white spruce, are dominant. The trees are shrouded with lichens, giving the forest a frosted appearance. Beneath the trees a thick carpet of feather moss envelops fallen trees and rocks. In lowland areas, such as around Grand Lake (Newfoundland's largest lake), trees grow to a fair size, and the timber obtained is of excellent quality. Mountain maples are abundant here, with white birch growing on burned-over sites. On exposed ridges, tuckamoor – tangled twisted thickets of stunted spruce and fir – form an impenetrable barrier. Extensive bogs and fens occur in low-lying areas. The northern part of the region is a transition from boreal forest to forest-tundra. Much of the land is covered by lichen-encrusted exposed rock. Fire has reduced much of the forest cover to scrublands dominated by alder, dwarf birch and Labrador tea.

WILDLIFE:

Great numbers of caribou thrive in this region. Caribou trails crisscross the high ridges and upland areas and provide erratic pathways through the tuckamoor. The extensive patches of lichens (caribou moss) provide important

Caribou

feeding areas, and the high rolling plateaux of the Long Range Mountains are nurseries where the caribou bear their young.

"Owing to the nutritive qualities of its super-excellent caribou moss, the deer [caribou] grow to a great size and in some respects throw out finer horns than any other form of the reindeer in existence. Big bucks sometimes weigh as much as 500 pounds."

J.G. Millais,
British sportsman and naturalist, 1900.

Introduced to Newfoundland in 1878 and subsequently in 1904, moose are abundant. Marten and wolves have been extirpated from the region, but marten have been reintroduced in Gros Morne National Park. The coastal strip lies along the Atlantic Flyway and provides important stopover sites for migrating waterfowl and shorebirds, as well as feeding areas for seabirds.

STATUS OF NATIONAL PARKS:

This region is represented by **Gros Morne National Park** (1943 km²). The Long Range Mountains, rising abruptly from the narrow coastal plain, dominate the park. The coastal plain is characterized by large raised bogs dotted with pitcher plants. The shoreline is extremely picturesque, varying from rocky headlands to broad sand beaches. Atop the Long Range Mountains is a vast alpine plateau of tundra, bogs and tuckamoor. The park is internationally acclaimed for its unique geological features. In addition to boasting over 30 fossil sites, this is one of the few places on the globe where rocks from deep within the earth are exposed. The entire southwestern portion of the park contains rocks from the earth's mantle (the layer surrounding the earth's molten core) and from the oceanic crust (the layer above the

Ten Mile Pond, Gros Morne National Park

Gros Morne National Park, Serpentine Tableland

A 1973 federal-provincial agreement, amended in 1983, with the Government of Newfoundland and Labrador provides for the establishment of the park. Currently, the harvest of wood for domestic use and snaring of snowshoe hares by local residents are permitted within selected areas of the park, as required by the federal-provincial agreement. Traditional renewable-resource harvesting regulations must be passed in order for Gros Morne to be proclaimed under the National Parks Act.

mantle). Much of the oceanic crustal material has eroded to expose the serpentine tableland, an unusual area of dark green rock which, because of its high magnesium content, stymies plant growth, creating a moonscape devoid of life.

Gros Morne has been named to the UNESCO List of World Heritage Sites for its awe-inspiring fiords and fiord-lakes and unique geological formations.

Gros Morne National Park, Lomond River

Cape St. Mary's

BOREAL BY THE SEA

...the country in all directions ... appeared to be covered with one dense unbroken pine forest, with here and there a bold granitic pap projecting above the dark-green surface .... Wind-fallen trees, underwood, and brooks lay in our way, which, together with the suffocating heat in the woods, and mosquitoes, hindered us from advancing more than five miles on this day....

William Cormack, 1822
The only known European to walk across Newfoundland

Terra Nova National Park

THE LAND:

The eroded remains of the ancient Appalachian Mountains give this region a rugged, hilly countenance. Along the coast in many places, sea cliffs rise precipitously 200-300 metres. Inland are innumerable lakes and rocky, fast-flowing rivers. The wounds left by the passing of the glaciers have not healed over much of the region. Large areas of exposed bedrock where the soil has been scraped away remain. Other areas are covered by glacial till. Lichen-encrusted erratic boulders perch on barren hilltops.

VEGETATION:

About one-half of the region is covered by a boreal forest of black spruce and balsam fir. Near the coast, an understory of feather moss thrives in the moist sea air. Inland, nearly pure stands of balsam fir occur on well-drained sites. In the hilly country and along protected valleys the forest is very productive and supports a thriving pulp-and-paper industry. Much of the original forest has been altered by human-caused fires. Bogs cover much of the region.

WILDLIFE:

"One of the most striking features of the interior is the innumerable deer-paths on the savannas. They ... take directions as various as the winds, giving the whole country a chequered appearance. Of the millions of acres here, there is no one spot exceeding a few superficial yards that is not bounded on all sides by deer-paths...."

William Cormack, 1822

Northwest River, Terra Nova National Park

Black-legged Kittiwake

Although the Strait of Belle Isle separating Newfoundland from the mainland is only 18 kilometres across, it has proven to be an effective barrier to many species of wildlife. Only 14 species of mammals are native to Newfoundland, compared to 42 species on the adjacent mainland. Many species, such as the moose, snowshoe hare

and red squirrel have been introduced and are now thriving. Some native species have only recently made the crossing. Lynx, for example, were not mentioned until the turn of the century. Other native species include the black bear, red fox, pine marten, beaver, mink and caribou. The wolf was once found here, but has been extirpated from the area. The caribou of Newfoundland are a unique sub-species and are the largest in North America.

Along the coastal cliffs and islands of this region are some of the largest seabird rookeries in North America. Cape St. Mary's and the Witless Bay Islands are two of the most accessible and spectacular seabird rookeries in the world. Hundreds of thousands of kittiwakes, puffins, gulls, common murres, razor-billed auks, gannets and millions of Leach's storm petrels breed at these sites. Important seabird colonies are protected as Migratory Bird Sanctuaries or Ecological Reserves. On visiting Funk Island in 1534, explorer Jacques Cartier extolled the abundance and fatness of the birds there. The flightless birds that Cartier was describing were great auks. They were hunted to extinction by 1844.

STATUS OF NATIONAL PARKS:

Terra Nova National Park (399 km^2) was established pursuant to a federal-provincial agreement in 1957. With its jagged rocky shorelines backed by dense boreal forest, the park protects an outstanding example of this natural

The Capelin are IN!

their curious deep crimson flowers conspicuous among the mainly pastel colours of the vegetation. Other plants that thrive in the acidic conditions found in bogs include Labrador tea, leatherleaf, bog laurel and sundews. The forest is dominated by black spruce and balsam fir. Much of the forest was logged before the park was established.

The wildlife found in the park is typical of this region. Caribou, once common in this part of Newfoundland, are still occasionally spotted. Moose, introduced to Newfoundland in 1878 and 1904, thrive and are often seen grazing in the park along the Trans-Canada highway. The Newfoundland pine marten has recently been reintroduced in Terra Nova National Park. The Terra Nova River provides fine fishing for Atlantic salmon and speckled trout.

region. The fiords or "sounds" that indent the coast are the park's most distinctive feature. Icebergs and whales can often be seen from the headlands framing the fiords. The teeming waters of Bonavista Bay and Newman Sound have attracted fishermen for hundreds of years, and some of Newfoundland's oldest settlements were located in the park.

Inland are numberless bogs and lakes filling depressions gouged out by the passing of glaciers during the Ice Age. Raised bogs, gentle domes rising about 1.5 metres above the surrounding terrain, are common. Sprouting from the sphagnum mosses and lichens are pitcher plants,

36 Western Arctic Lowlands

Not represented

Muskoxen

DOMAIN OF THE MUSKOX

Here I stand
Surrounded with great joy,
For the spirit of the air,
Lets glorious food sink down to me,
Here I stand"

song recorded on Victoria Island
by the Fifth Thule Expedition, 1924

THE LAND:

Low-lying, barren islands in the southwestern Arctic Archipelago distinguish this region. Victoria Island, the largest, is bigger than the four Atlantic provinces combined. The coastlines of these islands range from extensive lowlands to spectacular cliffs. Most of the area has been affected by the recent passage of the continental ice sheets. Fields of drumlins on southern Victoria Island impart a regular but complex "grain" that contrasts with the flat horizon of adjacent lowlands. Patches of undulating moraines, which appear from the air as gargantuan ploughed fields, break up vast plains where sinuous eskers provide the only vertical relief. Upland plateaux cut up into an Arctic version of badlands contrast with areas where nothing but broken limestone, sand and gravel are to be seen. Coal seams blacken the hills on Banks Island and loose chunks of coal are scattered on the beaches.

VEGETATION:

Most of this region is sparsely vegetated, with vast seemingly lifeless areas. Wet sites, however, have a heavy cover of sedges, cottongrass, mosses and saxifrages. In the southern fringes of the region, the thawed layer above the permafrost supports a thick layer of dwarf tundra shrubs. Dwarf birch, willow and alder can reach two metres in height. In windswept areas, trees – some as old as 400 years – grow horizontally, their branches twisted and convoluted and never rising more than a few centimetres above the soil.

Thomsen River, Banks Island

WILDLIFE:

In winter, this land appears to be almost empty of life. The summer cacophony of bird calls is gone. Of the large mammals, only muskoxen and caribou remain, steadfast in the face of the fiercest Arctic blizzards. Of the birds, only the raven, ptarmigan and a few snowy owls stay to face the cold and darkness. Beneath the snow, lemmings scurry along well-packed tunnels. But the surface of the land is still and silent.

Patterned Ground, Banks Island

In summer the land comes alive under the benevolence of 24-hour sunshine. Caribou and muskoxen get fat and bear their young in sheltered valleys. Flocks of snow geese and other waterfowl nest on the sedge meadows along river valleys.

STATUS OF NATIONAL PARKS:

The Thomsen River area on northern **Banks Island** was identified as a potential national park in 1978. This is an area of spectacular river canyons and desert-like badlands. The rolling

hills and lush valleys in the Thomsen River valley support the highest concentrations of muskoxen in the world.

All technical studies and initial planning work for the proposed park are complete. Consultations with residents of Sachs Harbour and the Government of the Northwest Territories are ongoing. Confirming local support for a national park will be an important step toward park establishment. This is largely dependent upon resolving the potential conflict with commercial muskox harvesting in the proposed park area.

Establishment of a national park in this natural region will require the support and co-operation of the residents of Sachs Harbour, the Inuvialuit and the Government of the Northwest Territories.

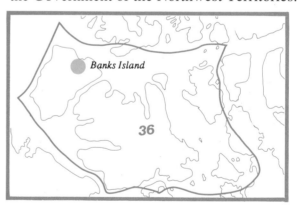

The following table summarizes the status of system planning for each step toward establishing a new national park in this natural region.

Steps in the Park Establishment Process	Status
Representative Natural Areas Identified:	done
Potential Park Areas Selected:	done
Park Feasibility Assessed:	in progress
Park Agreement Signed:	0
Scheduled Under the National Parks Act:	0

Muskox River Valley, Banks Island

Seabird Colony, Prince Leopold Island

GLORIOUS IT IS IN WINTER HERE!

**And yet there is only
One great thing,
The only thing,
To live to see in huts and on journeys
The great day that dawns
And the light that fills the world.**

Song recorded by the Fifth Thule Expedition, 1924

Hoodoos, Baffin Island

THE LAND:

In this region, sedimentary strata overlie Precambrian bedrock, resulting in low-lying plains and smooth plateaux, especially in the southern portions: "[the coast] is simply a ribbon of granite rising just above the high tide contour, at low water hemmed by ... a rocky tidal flat with a sprinkling of granite isles and reefs.... It was a desolate shore.... There seemed to be no elevations even 50 feet within a dozen miles of the coast." These were the words of explorer George Putnam in 1928.

Tidal flats over 10 kilometres wide are festooned with "growlers" and ice floes, sculpted into mushroom-like shapes by tide-driven waters. The two largest lakes in the Arctic Islands, Nettilling and Anadjuak, lie in the middle of the lowlands of southwestern Baffin Island. Inland is a flat country of marshy plains interspersed with bare rock, ponds and lakes.

The northern portions of the region present a contrast to the horizontal coastline and sodden lowlands of the south. The land rises abruptly to a high plateau. Several spectacular fiords slash inland, with sheer cliffs rising over 1000 metres.

The climate is bitterly cold, with overcast conditions prevailing much of the time. Precipitation is limited, creating desert conditions.

VEGETATION:

Vegetation is sparse, dwarfed and starved, particularly in the northern part of the region. Well-drained sites support a discontinuous cover of low-growing herbs and shrubs – sedges, saxifrages, willows, Dryas and arctic poppy are typical. In the southern lowlands, wet meadows of sedges, cottongrass and moss cover large areas.

WILDLIFE:

Although parts of this region support little wildlife, some areas are especially prolific. Large numbers of caribou, wolf, arctic fox, wolverine, collared lemming and arctic hare are found in fertile areas of the land and sea. Polar bears use the coastal areas for winter denning and spring seal hunting.

King Elder

The wet lowland meadows adjacent to Hudson Bay and Foxe Basin and the lake-studded coastal plain of western Baffin Island provide the most important habitat for waterfowl in the entire Arctic. The largest goose colony in the Arctic is found here, on the Koudjuak Plain. Over one million lesser snow geese, Canada geese and brant nest and feed on the marshy sedge tundra of the plain in summer. King eider, common eider, oldsquaw and brant are the most abundant nesting species.

Prince Leopold Island

STATUS OF NATIONAL PARKS:

The **Bylot Island/North Baffin** area has been studied intensively as a proposed national park. The scenery of the entire area is impressive: sea cliffs over 300 metres, glaciers dropping into the sea, high mountains and some of the world's most spectacular fiords. The concentration of marine mammals and birds in the area is remarkable. Several huge cliff colonies of seabirds are found along the coast of Lancaster Sound and northern Baffin Island, including a colony of over 400,000 thick-billed murres, along with black-legged kittiwakes, arctic terns and northern fulmars. Bylot Island supports about 35 percent of the world's breeding population of greater snow geese. In the waters adjacent to the proposed park area, narwhals, belugas, walrus, polar bear and five species of seal (harbour, hooded, bearded, harp and ringed) abound. The rare bowhead whale regularly frequents Lancaster Sound.

In 1987 the Canadian Parks Service initiated formal public consultations regarding a proposal to create a side-by-side national park and national marine park in the Bylot Island/North Baffin area. Consultations to date indicate that local support is lacking for a national marine park. Stronger community interest exists for a national park, however, and consultations are continuing. The settlement terms of the Tungavik Federation of Nunavut comprehensive claim will affect park establishment.

Establishment of a national park in this natural region will require the support and co-operation of the residents of Arctic Bay and Pond Inlet, the Tungavik Federation of Nunavut and the Government of the Northwest Territories.

The following table summarizes the status of system planning for each step toward establishing a new national park in this natural region.

Bylot Island

Steps in the Park Establishment Process	Status
Representative Natural Areas Identified:	done
Potential Park Areas Selected:	done
Park Feasibility Assessed:	in progress
Park Agreement Signed:	0
Scheduled Under the National Parks Act:	0

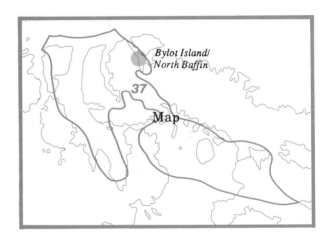

38 Western High Arctic

Not represented

ISLANDS IN A FROZEN SEA

The silence hangs so deep that time itself seems to stand still. Stand on a ridge like thousands of others on an island like dozens of others and in all directions there is only stillness and peace. Only the wind moves.

Polar Bears

THE LAND:

This is a region of the sea – nowhere in this region of islands can you stand more than 50 kilometres from the sea. Yet despite its proximity to the water, most of this region is polar desert – a frigid, barren rock-strewn land. It is one of the driest regions in the world, receiving less than 11 centimetres of precipitation yearly. Snow may fall in any month, a dry powdery snow that blows like dust on the wind. It accumulates in ravines and valleys where it forms hard packed drifts that have the consistency of Styrofoam.

Each island that makes up this region has its own character ranging from flat to rugged. The mountains on Melville Island, the largest, reach heights of one kilometre. In contrast, the southwest part of Bathurst Island is a remarkably flat sand and gravel plain.

The north magnetic pole is located in this region.

VEGETATION:

Much of this region has little or no vegetation. Where continuous vegetation occurs, it usually consists of hummocks of mosses, lichens, grasses and sedges. The only woody species, the dwarf willow, grows as a dense twisted mat crawling along the ground. Vast areas appear completely devoid of life from a distance. But lichens and mosses cover the rocks; grasses grow around meltwater puddles, and the hilltops bare of snow are tinted with the warm living shades of red and brown.

WILDLIFE:

For a region sparse in plant life, it boasts a surprising number of animals; polar bear, Peary caribou, musk-ox, collared lemming, arctic wolf, arctic fox, arctic hare and ermine in small, discontinuous populations concentrated around wet lowlands. Life is tenuous in this region. An early snowfall that melts and then freezes, sealing vegetation beneath a layer of ice, can spell disaster.

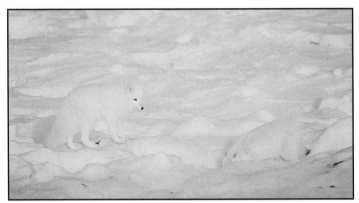
Arctic Foxes

provide nesting habitat for myriads of shorebirds and waterfowl: black-bellied plovers, knots, pectoral sandpipers, king eiders, greater snow geese, brant, oldsquaw and red-throated loon, among others.

The only known nesting site of the ivory gull is found in this region and is protected as Seymour Island Migratory Bird Sanctuary (8 km²).

Birds are more fortunate. They can fly away when times are rough. Snowy owls depend on lemmings as a food source. But lemming populations fluctuate on a four to seven-year cycle. Luckily for the owls, each island is at a different phase of the cycle, meaning that they can simply fly off to another island where the hunting is good. The arctic foxes are not so lucky.

Birds abound here in summer, especially on the southern islands. The valleys and lowlands, bespeckled with meltwater ponds and puddles,

Polar Bear Pass National Wildlife Area, Bathurst Island

STATUS OF NATIONAL PARKS:

Two representative natural areas have been identified: **Bjorne Peninsula** (Ellesmere Island) and **Central Bathurst Island**. Much of the latter area is protected as **Polar Bear Pass National Wildlife Area** (2624 km²). A Ramsar site (a wetland of international significance), Polar Bear Pass is the first National Wildlife Area in the North and is protected under the regulations of the Canada Wildlife Act. Vast numbers of king eider, greater snow geese, gulls, jaegers and shorebirds (especially sanderlings) nest here, and it is an important calving and wintering area for musk-oxen. Polar bears regularly traverse the pass in spring and summer. The pass itself is a 65-kilometre-long lowland bisecting Bathurst Island. The vegetation is diverse and lush for this northern latitude.

The Bjorne Peninsula is an area of rolling upland hills and sharp ridges that are representative of the abiotic components of the region. Although valleys and wet areas support lush mosses and meadows, the majority of the area is sparsely vegetated. The highlands of the northern portions of the area, north of the Sydkap Icecap, are almost totally devoid of plant life. Small mammals, such as hare and lemming, are common. Caribou and muskoxen occur, but their populations are not large.

The next step will be to consider whether one of these areas should be selected for further study as a potential national park.

Establishment of a national park in this natural region will require the support and co-operation of the Tungavik Federation of Nunavut and/or the Inuvialuit and the Government of the Northwest Territories.

Bjorne Peninsula

The following table summarizes the status of system planning for each step toward establishing a new national park in this natural region.

Steps in the Park Establishment Process	Status
Representative Natural Areas Identified:	done
Potential Park Areas Selected:	0
Park Feasibility Assessed:	0
Park Agreement Signed:	0
Scheduled Under the National Parks Act:	0

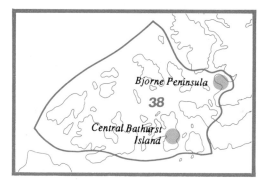

39 Eastern High Arctic Glacier

Represented by: Ellesmere Island National Park Reserve

Tanquary Fiord, Ellesmere Island National Park Reserve

TOP OF THE WORLD

This is as far away as you can get in Canada. Here is a land of desolation and splendor on a grand scale. But it is also a land of intimate, fragile beauty – of delicate arctic poppies vibrating in the breeze, of miniature forests of lichens and heather, of subtle pastel shades and heady aromas.

THE LAND:

Most of this region is desert – a lifeless frozen land. The Ice Age still holds sway over this land, and massive ice caps cloak much of this region. On Ellesmere Island, the ice cap is 2100 metres above sea level and hundreds of metres thick. The rugged peaks of the Innuitian Mountains, among the highest in Canada, pierce the ice. Like hands groping to touch, glaciers extend icy fingers

Signing Ceremony, Ellesmere Island National Park Reserve

toward fiords reaching inland.

Along Ellesmere Island's northern coast, ice shelves, permanent aprons of ice held fast to the shore for thousands of years, cover vast areas of the Arctic Ocean.

The climate is "damn" cold. Even in July, the largely ice-covered seas refrigerate the land. The region is dry, receiving about the same precipitation as the Sahara.

VEGETATION:

Although most of the region is ice and rock, there are a few areas, called Arctic thermal oases, that have remarkably high biological productivity for the latitude. Although they cover less than two percent of the land, they are of critical importance to all life in the region. During the brief summer of continuous 24-hour sunlight, these oases burst into bloom in a frantic rush to complete life cycles before the onset of winter. In the most luxuriant oases, heathers and blueberries are found. More common are meadows of sedges and mosses, along with herbs that grow in dense cushions and mats. The entrances to animal dens, the ground around decomposed carcasses, old campsites and other "fertilized" spots stand out as having lusher, more colourful vegetation than the surrounding areas.

WILDLIFE:

This region has few species of animals. Land mammals include Peary caribou, muskox, wolf, arctic fox, ermine, arctic hare and collared lemming. Conspicuous land birds include the horned lark, hoary redpoll, snow bunting and willow ptarmigan. Peary caribou are smaller and paler than barren-ground caribou. Unlike their mainland relatives, they do not undertake long seasonal

Peary Caribou

migrations or travel in huge herds. They occur in small scattered groups, sometimes in the most seemingly inhospitable habitats. Severe winters in recent years have caused the number of Peary Caribou to drop alarmingly.

Analogous to the terrestrial oases, marine "oases" – areas of high productivity – harbour rich populations of marine mammals on the fringe of the terrestrial region – polar bear, walrus, ringed and bearded seals, and narwhals congregate in certain areas such as Lancaster Sound. Several large seabird rookeries are located near these rich feeding sites. Thick-billed murres, black-legged kittiwakes, northern fulmars, black guillemots, Thayer's gulls and glaucous gulls are the most common species.

Snow geese, eiders, oldsquaw and a host of shorebirds nest on the grassy tundra. The arctic tern also nests here on the shores of lakes and along beaches. This champion migrator follows the sun of summer, never knowing a day of winter in its life.

STATUS OF NATIONAL PARKS:

Ellesmere Island National Park Reserve (37 775 km²), Canada's second largest national park, represents this natural region. A land of ice, it is dominated by hundreds of glaciers. Mount Barbeau (2600 m), the highest mountain in eastern North America, towers over vast ice fields. The long bitterly cold winters, brief cool summers and low precipitation have created polar desert conditions throughout much of the park, with little vegetation or wildlife. However, lowland areas, such as the one surrounding Lake Hazen, the most northerly lake in Canada, are relatively lush. In these thermal oases, arctic hare often congregate in groups of hundreds. Small herds of muskoxen and Peary caribou, a few

Lake Hazen

Ward Hunt Ice Shelf

The agreement between the federal government and the Government of the Northwest Territories setting out the terms and conditions for establishing Ellesmere Island National Park Reserve was signed in 1986. The historic signing ceremony took place on a snowy September day on the shores of Tanquary Fiord. Flags snapped and and a lone arctic hare hopped by as the coldest park agreement signing ceremony in the history of national park establishment took place. The lands are subject to settlement of the Tungavik Federation of Nunavut comprehensive claim. Local native people advise on the planning and management of the park reserve.

wolves, numerous arctic foxes and about 30 species of birds thrive in meadows of lush grasses and bright arctic flowers.

Hundreds of archaeological sites in the park tell of ancient Inuit peoples who passed this way 4000 years ago. The remains of Fort Conger, a scientific research base established in 1881, is a site of historic significance. Wooden shacks built by the Arctic explorer Robert Peary, of North Pole fame, still stand on the site.

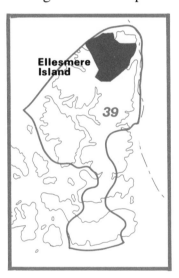

Table I — Status of National Regions

National Region	Location	National Park(s) present and/or needed	Areas of Interest Identified/comments	Other Significant Protected Areas	Comments
1. Pacific Coast Mountains	BC	Pacific Rim N.P. Reserve (500 km^2)	Fed-prov agreements 1970/1987	Strathcona Pr. Pk. (2112 km^2) Tweedsmuir Pr. Pk. (9811 km^2) Garibaldi Pr. Pk. (1943 km^2) Naikoon Pr. Pk. (726 km^2) Cape Scott Pr. Pk. (150 km^2) Cathedral Pr. Pk. (336 km^2) Manning Pr. Pk. (714 km^2)	BC's oldest Half in N.R. 3 Includes Black Tusk Nature Conservancy
		South Moresby/ Gwaii Haanas N.P. Reserve (1470 km^2)	1988: Fed-prov agreement ; includes Ninstints, a IUCN World Heritage Site	43 ecological reserves totalling 912 km^2	
2. Strait of Georgia Lowlands	BC	needed	Regional analysis study needed	Desolation Sound Pr. Pk. (85 km^2) Alaksen NWA/MBS	Over 50 small coastal ad marine prov. parks; 16 ecological reserves Ramsar site
3. Dry Interior Plateau	BC	needed	Churn Creek Fraser-Chilcoten Junction	Tweedsmuir Pr. Pk. 33 ecological reserves totalling 119 km^2	Half in N.R. 1
4. Coloumbia Moutains	BC	Glacier N.P. (1349 km^2) Mt. Revelstoke N.P. (259 km^2)	Proclaimed 1886 Proclaimed 1914	Wells Grey Pr. Pk. (5273 km^2) Bowron Lakes Pr. Pk. (1231 km^2)	Includes Murtle Lake Nature Conservancy
5. Rocky Moutains	BC Alta	Banff N.P. (6641 km^2) Yoho N.P. (1313 km^2) Waterton Lakes N.P. (505 km^2) Jasper N.P. (10 787 km^2) Kootenay N.P. (1406 km^2)	Proclaimed 1885 Proclaimed 1886 Proclaimed 1895 – part of Biosphere Reserve Proclaimed 1907 Proclaimed 1920 Banff, Jasper, Kooteney and Yoho collectively comprise Rocky Mountains World Heritage Site	Mt. Robson Pr. Pk. (2198 km^2) Kwadacha Wilderness (1675 km^2) Muncho Lake Pr. Pk. (889 km^2) Mt. Assiniboine Pr. Pk. (391 km^2) Willmore Wilderness Pk. (4597 km^2) White Goat Wilderness Area (443 km^2) Siffleur Wilderness Area (418 km^2) Ghost River Wilderness Area (397 km^2) Athabasca Canadian Heritage River (168 km corridor) North Saskatchewan Canadian Heritage River (49 km corridor) Kicking Horse Canadian Heritage River (67 km corridor)	BC BC BC BC Alta Alta Alta Alta

National Region	Location	National Park(s) present and/or needed	Areas of Interest Identified/comments	Other Significant Protected Areas	Comments
6. Northern Coast Mountains	BC YT	Kluane N.P. Reserve (22 015 km²)	Proclaimed 1972 World Heritage Site	Atlin Pr. Pk. (2711 km²) Alsek Canadian Heritage River (90 km corridor)	BC; part in N.R. 7
7. Northern Interior Mountains and Plateaux	BC YT	needed	Spatsizi Plateau (BC) Mt. Edziza (BC) Yukon River-Southern Ogilvies (YT) Kluane-Aishihik (YT)	Spatsizi Plateau Wilderness Pr. Pk. (6597 km²) Mount Edziza Pr. Pk. (1319 km²) Tatlatui Pr. Pk. (1058 km²) Atlin Pr. Pk. Yukon Canadian Heritage River (48 km corridor)	BC (includes Gladys Lake Ecological Res. where no sport hunting is allowed) BC BC BC
8. MacKenzie Mountains	NWT YT	Nahanni N.P. Reserve (4766 km²)	Proclaimed in 1976; expansion of present boundaries being considered; World Heritage Site	South Nahanni Canadian Heritage River (300 km corridor)	
9. Northern Yukon	YT	Northern Yukon N.P. (10 168 km²)	Proclaimed 1984 – additional representation needed; Old Crow Flats (Ramsar Site) is candidate for an adjacent PP	none	
10. MacKenzie Delta	NWT YT	Northern Yukon N.P.	2400 km² of total park (see N.R. 9)	Herschel Island Territorial Pk. (101 km²)	YT's first Territorial Park
11. Northern Boreal Plains	NWT YT Alta	Wood Buffalo N.P. (44 807 km²)	NWT/Alta Proclaimed 1922; Extends slightly into NR 12, 17; World Heritage Site Ramsar Site	none	
12. Southern Boreal Plains	BC Alta Sask NWT Man	Wood Buffalo N.P. Riding Mt. N.P. (2976 km²) Elk Island N.P. (194 km²) Prince Albert N.P. (3875 km²)	8% of total park (see NR 11); Proclaimed 1929; Man. Biosphere Reserve Proclaimed 1913 Alta. Proclaimed 1927 Sask.	Duck Mt. Pr. Pk. (262 km²) Clearwater River Wilderness (2240 km²) Nipawin Pr. Pk. (536 km²) Meadow Lake Pr. Pk. (1570 km²) Duck Mt. Pr. Pk. (1274 km²) Clearwater Canadian Heritage River (187 km corridor)	Sask Sask Sask Sask Man

National Region	Location	National Park(s) present and/or needed	Areas of Interest Identified/comments	Other Significant Protected Areas	Comments
13. Prairie Grasslands	Man Sask Alta	Grasslands N.P. (906 km²)	Fed-prov agreements 1981/88; not yet proclaimed Sask	Dinosaur Pr. Pk. Cypress Hills Pr. Pk. (184 km²) Cypress Hills Pr. Pk. (205 km²) Turtle Mt. Pr. Pk. (189km²) Last Mountain Lake MBS Ramsar Site	Alta IUCN World Heritage Site Sask Alta Man Sask; Ramsar Site
14. Manitoba Lowlands	Man Sask	needed	Long Point (Man); Little Limestone Lake (Man) Hecla (Man)	Grass River Pr. Pk. (1148 km²) Hecla (863 km²) Delta Marsh Wildlife Area Oak-Hammock Marsh Wildlife Area	Man Man Ramsar Site Ramsar Site
15. Tundra Hills	NWT	needed	Bluenose Lake		
16. Central Tundra	NWT	needed	Wager Bay	Thelon Game Sanctuary (55 000 km²) Thelon Canadian Heritage River (545 km corridor) Kazan Canadian Heritage River (615 km corridor) Queen Maud Gulf MBS (62 000 km²) McConnell River MBS East Bay MBS	 Ramsar Site Ramsar Site
17. Northwestern Boreal Uplands	NWT Man Sask	needed	East Arm of Great Slave Lake/Artillery Lake	Seal Canadian Heritage River (260 km corridor)	
18. Central Boreal Uplands	Sask Man Ont PQ	Pukaskwa N.P. (1878 km²)	Est. 1978; not yet proclaimed Ont	Atikaki Wilderness Pr. Pk. (4668 km²) Kesagami Wilderness Pr. Pk. (560 km²) Opasquia Wilderness Pr. Pk. (4730 km²) Woodland Caribou Wilderness Pr. Pk. (4500 km²) Wabakimi Wilderness Pr. Pk. (150 km²) Aiguebelle Pr. Pk. (241 km²) Bloodvein Canadian Heritage River (300 km corridor) Missinaibi Canadian Heritage RIver (426 km corridor)	Man Ont Ont Ont Ont PQ

National Region	Location	National Park(s) present and/or needed	Areas of Interest Identified/comments	Other Significant Protected Areas	Comments
19. Great Lakes – St. Lawrence Precambrian	Man Ont PQ	Georgian Bay Islands (25 km²) La Mauricie N.P. (544 km²) St. Lawrence Islands N.P. (6 km²)	Proclaimed 1929 Proclaimed 1970 Proclaimed 1914	Lady Evelyn Smoothwater Wilderness Pr. Pk. (724 km²) Mont-Tremblant Pr. Pk. (1240 km²) Quetico Wilderness Pr. Pk. (4758 km²) Saquenay Pr. Pk. (283 km²) Killarney Wilderness Pr. Pk. (485 km²) Lake Superior Pr. Pk. (1556 km²) Algonquin Pr. Pk. (7653 km²) French Canadian Heritage River (110 km corridor) Mattawa Canadian Heritage River (33 km corridor) Boundary Waters Canadian Heritage Waterway (250 km corridor) Jaques Cartier Canadian Heritage River (128 km corridor)	Ont PQ Ont PQ Ont Ont Ont Canada's oldest Pr. Pk.
20. Laurentian Boreal Highlands	PQ	needed	regional study needed	Jacques Cartier Pr. Pk. (670 km²) Grands Jardins Pr. Pk. (310 km²) Jacques Cartier Canadian Heritage River (part) Charlevoix Biosphere Reserve Cap Tourmente MBS	Ramsar site
21. East Coast Boreal	Nfld PQ	needed	Mealy Mountains	none	
22. Boreal Lake Plateau	PQ	needed	Richmond Gulf	none	
23. Whale River	PQ	needed	George River Caniapiscau River Koksoak River	none	
24. Northern Labrador Mountains	Nfld	needed	Torngat Mountains	none	
25. Ungava Tundra Plateau	PQ NWT	needed	Leaf River (PQ) Nastapoka (NWT/PQ)	none	
26. Northern Davis	NWT	Auyuittuq N.P. Reserve (27 471 km²)	Proclaimed 1976	Bylot Island MBS (10 878 km²) Cape Dorset MBS (259 km²)	

National Region	Location	National Park(s) present and/or needed	Areas of Interest Identified/comments	Other Significant Protected Areas	Comments
27. Hudson-James Lowlands	Man Ont NWT PQ	needed	Cape Churchill/York Factory	Polar Bear Wilderness Pr. Pk. (24 087km^2) Akimiski Island MBS (3367 km^2) Twin Islands Wildlife Sanctuary (1425 km^2)	Ont Ramsar site NWT NWT
28. Southampton Plain	NWT	needed	regional analysis needed	Harry Gibbons MBS (1489 km^2)	
29. St. Lawrence Lowlands	Ont PQ Nfld	Georgian Bay Islands N.P. Bruce Peninsula N.P. (270 km^2) Point Pelee N.P. (16 km^2) Mingan Archipelago N.P. Reserve (151 km^2)	small portion of total park (see NR 19) Fed-prov agreement 1987; not yet proclaimed Ont.; Ramsar Site; proclaimed 1918 Ont PQ; proclaimed 1984	Mont St. Hilaire (PQ) Grand Canadian Heritage River (Ont 290 km corridor) Long Point NWA (Ont) St. Clair NWA (Ont) Niagara Biosphere Reserve Lac St. Francois NWA	Biosphere Reserve Ramsar Site; Biosphere Reserve Ramsar Site Ont PQ; Ramsar site
30. Notre-Dame and Megantic Mountains	PQ NB	Forillon N.P.	PQ; proclaimed 1970	Mount Carleton Pr. Pk. (174 km^2) Gaspesie Pr. Pk. (802 km^2) Cap Toumente NWA Baie de l'Isle Verte NWA	NB PQ Ramsar site Ramsar site
31. Maritime Acadian Highlands	NB NS	Fundy N.P. (206 km^2) Cape Breton Highlands N.P. (951 km^2)	NS; proclaimed 1948 NS; proclaimed 1936	Shepody Bay NWA Chignecto NWA South Bight-Minas Basin Fortress of Louisbourg National Historic Park (67 km^2)	NB; Ramsar site NS; Ramsar site NS; Ramsar site
32. Maritime Plain	NB NS PEI	Prince Edward Island N.P. (26 km^2) Kouchibouguac N.P. (239 km^2)	Proclaimed 1937 NB; proclaimed 1979	Malpeque River Bay Wildlife Management Area (24 km^2)	PEI; Ramsar site
33. Atlantic Coast Uplands	NS	Kejimkujik N.P. (384 km^2)	Proclaimed 1967 Port Mouton coastal adjunct added 1988	Musquodoboit Harbour Wildlife Management Area (24 km^2)	NS; Ramsar site
34. Western Nfld Highlands	Nfld	Gros Morne N.P. (1943 km^2)	Fed-prov agreements 1973/83 World Heritage Site	Codroy Valley River Pr. Pk.	Ramsar site
35. Eastern Nfld Atlantic	Nfld	Terra Nova N.P. (399 km^2)	Proclaimed 1957	Bay du Nord Wilderness Reserve (3455 km^2) Avalon Wilderness Reserve (1070 km^2)	

National Region	Location	National Park(s) present and/or needed	Areas of Interest Identified/comments	Other Significant Protected Areas	Comments
36. Western Artic Lowlands	NWT	needed	Thomsen River (Northern Banks Island)	Banks Island No. 1 MBS (20 518 km^2) Banks Island No. 2 MBS (142 km^2)	
37. Eastern Arctic Lowlands	NWT	needed	Bylot Island/North Baffin	Dewey Soper MBS (8159 km^2)	
38. Western High Arctic	NWT	needed	Bjorne Peninsula Central Bathurst Island	Polar Bear Pass NWA (2624 km^2)	Ramsar Site
39. Eastern High Arctic Glacier	NWT	Ellesmere Island N.P. Reserve (37 775 km^2)	Fed-terr agreement 1986		

MBS = Migratory Bird Sanctuary
NWA = National Wildlife Area
Ramsar Site = Wetland of International Significance
N.P. = National Park
Pr. Pk. = Provincial Park